CONQUERING UNCERTAINTY

Mastering the Art of Creative Collaboration
Robert Hargrove

TransCompetition
Harvey Robbins and Michael Finley

The Market Makers
Daniel F. Spulber

CONQUERING UNCERTAINTY

Understanding Corporate
Cycles and Positioning
Your Company to Survive
the Changing Environment

Theodore Modis

 **BusinessWeek Books**

McGraw-Hill
New York   San Francisco   Washington, D.C.   Auckland   Bogotá
Caracas   Lisbon   London   Madrid   Mexico City   Milan
Montreal   New Delhi   San Juan   Singapore
Sydney   Tokyo   Toronto

Library of Congress Cataloging-in-Publication Data

Modis, Theodore.
    Conquering uncertainty : understanding corporate cycles and
positioning your company to survive the changing environment /
Theodore Modis.
        p.   cm.
    Includes bibliographical references (p.) and index.
    ISBN 0-07-043405-0
    1. Industrial management.   2. Industrial organization.
3. Business cycles.   4. Technological innovations.   I. Title.
HD31.M6143   1998
658.4'06—dc21   97-49364
                                                                        CIP

McGraw-Hill

A Division of The McGraw·Hill Companies

1 2 3 4 5 6 7 8 9 0   DOC/DOC   9 0 3 2 1 0 9 8

ISBN 0-07-043405-0

*The editing supervisor was Caroline Levine and the production
supervisor was Sherri Souffrance. This book was set in Fairfield by
Victoria Khavkina of McGraw-Hill's Professional Book Group
composition unit.*

Printed and bound by R. R. Donnelley & Sons Company.

McGraw-Hill books are available at special quantity discounts to use
as premiums and sales promotions, or for use in corporate training
programs. For more information, please write to the Director of
Special Sales, McGraw-Hill, 11 West 19th Street, New York, NY
10011. Or contact your local bookstore.

This book is printed on recycled, acid-free paper containing
a minimum of 50% recycled, de-inked fiber.

To Yorgo and Thea

CONTENTS

Preface   *xi*
Acknowledgments   *xv*

PROLOGUE   1

Academic Too Often Means Useless   *4*
Growth Dynamics   *6*

CHAPTER ONE. THE S-SHAPED ADVENTURE   9

What Do Computers and Rabbits Have in Common?   *13*
Just-in-Time Innovation   *24*

**CHAPTER TWO. STRUCTURING AN ENTERPRISE
ACCORDING TO ITS SEASON**   27

The Four Seasons of a Business Cycle   *29*
   Second Thoughts about Excellence   *33*
   Winter   *34*
   Spring   *36*
   Summer   *37*
   Fall   *38*
   Like Shakespearean Plays   *42*
The BCG Matrix Revisited   *43*
Where Are You on the Curve?   *46*
Gedanken Experiments   *51*
Leonardo da Vinci Was Ahead of the Aristocrats   *53*

**CHAPTER THREE. GROWTH FROM CHAOS AND
CHAOS FROM GROWTH**   57

The Beginning of Chaos   *58*

A Large-Scale Historical Example   60
In Politics as in Business   65
The Collapse of the Communist Empire   66
The Rise and Fall of a Computer Giant   67
Revolutions and Re-Evolutions   71
If Summer Is Here, Can Fall Be Far Behind?   73
Where on the Curve Are Your Clients?   75
Success in All Seasons   78
   The Philosopher's Stone   80
   Examples   81

CHAPTER FOUR. THE BIG PICTURE   83

The Evolution of the Evolution   83
Zooming in and out   88
Examples from Industry   93
Showing off at the Dock   96
When Do We Stop Being Children?   97
The End of the Information-Technology Industry   98
   No More Downsizing in Computers   99
   Personal Computers Are Not Getting Cheaper   100

CHAPTER FIVE. INSTINCT VERSUS RATIONALE   103

Assess, Measure, and Monitor Strategic Performance   104
Could You Take Aim at an Apple on Your Son's Head?   107
Learning from Experience in Positioning New Computer
  Products   109
The Industry Learning Curve   113
Life Cycles of Services   114

CHAPTER SIX. GENETIC RE-ENGINEERING
OF CORPORATIONS   117

More than One Species in the Same Niche   118
Attacker's Advantage, Defender's Counterattack   119
Competition Management   124
Finding the Magic Advertising Message   127
Who Is Afraid of the Big Bad Wolf?   132

CHAPTER SEVEN. MAKE THE FUTURE WHAT IT USED TO BE   135

Invariants   *138*
   The Nonsense about Safe Driving   *139*
   Humans Versus Machines   *142*
Decision Nonmakers   *144*
Did Mozart Die of Old Age?   *149*
A Second Lease on Life   *153*

CHAPTER EIGHT. MANAGING THE ENTERPRISE AFTER YEAR 2000   159

EPILOGUE   165

APPENDIX A. S-CURVES: MATHEMATICAL FORMULATIONS   169

One Species Only   *169*
Many Competitors in a Niche   *171*

APPENDIX B. ECONOMIES OF SCALE AND PRICE ELASTICITY   173

Why the Industrial Revolution Succeeded   *174*

NOTES AND SOURCES   *177*

BIBLIOGRAPHY   *185*

Index   *189*

PREFACE

This book is about anticipating the future of your business and taking action successfully despite relentless change. You can understand the evolution of your business before the fact. Moreover, a bigger picture may reveal surprises; for example, when freedom of action seems limited, you may be in a period where limited activity is *appropriate* and need not be a source of frustration.

The book was written in response to such remarks as

- The future is unpredictable.
- The rate of change is accelerating.
- Who would ever have imagined that . . .
- The future is no longer what it used to be.

Alarmists—always vocal—react to the unease expressed by such remarks by predicting imminent doom. While it is true that change breeds instability and feelings of insecurity, society has long managed to evolve with ever-increasing average prosperity and well-being for human beings on a global scale.

It is possible to predict events in business and prepare for situations successfully *while* change is taking place at an accelerating rate. I will show that change is *not* rampant, random, and unpredictable. There is logic to the madness. There are fundamental laws that govern "random" change.

NATURAL LAWS

Natural laws have always been the basis of my thinking. I was trained as a physicist and for many years carried out research in particle accelerator laboratories. Some of these natural laws have persisted at the center of my thinking, playing a prominent role guiding me during the 15 years since I left an academic career to work first as a management science consultant at Digital Equipment Corporation and later as futurist and strategist. *Fundamental* concepts, such as equilibrium, competition, feedback, and survival of the fittest, are notions encountered in the marketplace daily.

Equilibrium is typically what happens when supply meets demand. The right price falls out as a by-product of this phenomenon. *Feedback* can be responsible for oscillations; for example, when demand signals for a newly launched product are overinterpreted. *Competition* intensifies as the market niche becomes saturated; this provokes the downturn on the product's sales life cycle. *Survival of the fittest* determines who will be predator and who prey. The market is full of competitors acting in one or the other capacity.

TREATING PRODUCTS LIKE SPECIES

My first attempt to apply ideas from the natural sciences to the marketplace was to treat products like species, with the focus on life cycle, market penetration, and product substitution. This approach was extended to families of products, technologies, markets, and similar growth processes that are subject to competition. Then, it was possible to focus on the various stages of the product or technology life cycle and finally to understand intercompany competition and the strategies that will sustain growth over prolonged periods.

CHAOS IS SEASONAL

Certain events appear to occur in an irregular sequence of nonrepeating patterns. Such a picture, which corresponds to the scientific notion of *chaos*, may seem to be useless in preparing for the future. But chaos in business, like many other phenomena, appears to be *seasonal*. In particular, chaos is associated with low-growth business seasons. Once a business gets into a high-growth season, events become more orderly. Moreover, *good business seasons alternate with bad business seasons, implying that chaos eventually leads to order and vice versa.* There is "harmony" in this swing from chaos to order and back, which can be utilized in preparing for future events.

PREPARING FOR FUTURE EVENTS

This book is about the actions that must be taken when facing up to a seasonal change in business. Actions must be adapted to the economic climate to ensure survival. Low-growth, seemingly chaotic days demand horizontal structures, entrepreneurship, and innovation. Early growth periods need investment. Rapid growth responds to a more "vertical" approach. In other words, there is a seaon for leaders and a season for entrepreneurs, a time for specialists, and, surprisingly, a time for bureaucrats. Reengineering, total quality, and benchmarking all have a time when they are best—like oranges in winter and watermelons in summer. Creativity and innovation are not the first priority at all times, just as total quality must take second place while searching for new directions.

KEY TO A SUCCESSFUL STRATEGY

Seeing events and actions to be taken as a function of time is the key to a successful strategy. The seasonal dimension can be imposed on all business activity. Birth implies death. A business life cycle has different stages, each governed by its own rules. Those who follow these rules will grow in harmony and along the path of least resistance. To follow these rules two key pieces of information are needed:

- Where in the growth process is your business? What "season" is it in?
- What is the time frame for the growth, decay, and rebirth of your business?

This book will enable the reader to answer these questions.

Theodore Modis

ACKNOWLEDGMENTS

This book has benefited from contributions and discussions with many individuals. Among them, special mention must be given to three people: Cesare Marchetti, who introduced me to this field that now has become my *raison d'être*; Michael Royston, who advised, coached, and encouraged me in a whole-hearted way; and Nikos Nikas, my lifelong friend and classmate from high school, who lent time and painstaking effort both with the manuscript and with emotional support. Credit must also be given to those who have directly contributed to the content, namely Professors Carl Pistorius from the University of Pretoria, Thanasis Konstandopoulos from the University of Thessaloniki, Alain Debecker from the University of Lyon, and Mihali Yannopoulos.

I would like to thank several other people who read and commented on the manuscript: Fred Neubauer, Phil Bagwell, Eigil Kiste, John Geesing, Candy Mirrer, Daniel Ducret, Robert Posey, and Juan Rada. The manuscript benefited as well from editorial work by Marilyn Gildea and logistic and software support by Rodica Antonescu.

Finally, I want to thank my agent, Hans Ritman, for his energetic and entrepreneurial support, and my editors at McGraw-Hill, Mary Glenn and Caroline Levine, who worked hard to make the text easily understandable for the reader.

Theodore Modis

PROLOGUE

The thesis is simple. Most people in positions of authority, whether in government, business, the third sector, or international organizations, simply don't know what they are doing when they respond to change.

"This is an audacious statement," I said to myself as I read it, "and yet it resonates with my own experience." I was reading an article by Joseph Coates, from the futurist consulting firm Coates & Jarratt.[1] His argument was that people of authority usually have inadequate command of the range of alternatives before them and generally lack full understanding of the situation, whether it is a problem or a potential opportunity. As a rule they have no means of gaining insight into all the consequences of their actions, and they often see an unnecessarily restricted range of choices. But all this is not caused by ignorance, wrongdoing, stupidity, or incompetence. The relationship of policies to interdependencies is too complex to be reliably analyzed by discussion and intuition. This is why the case method of management education has had limited success, argues Jay Forrester at MIT.[2] The case method has achieved a wide following, but it is plagued by the risk of drawing the wrong dynamic conclusions and fails to explain why corporations in apparently similar situations can behave so differently. It is intrinsically impossible to anticipate all important outcomes. A systematic procedure of general validity is therefore needed on how to approach decision making when confronted with change.

The quest for a philosopher's stone—a kind of Aladdin's

lantern that will always tell you the right thing to do—has drawn energy and time from me since I was a teenager. As a professional I became involved with data analysis and experimentation as well as strategic planning and forecasting. For the last 12 years I have been exploring ways to unearth predictability, obtain new insights, and develop techniques and tools that will enable senior executives to assess, measure, and monitor their strategies. By accident—or fate—my activities have evolved from extracting scientific knowledge via physics experiments to exploring new ways of thinking in strategic management. In both areas my contribution has been to see patterns where other people did not. I have concluded that despite a turmoil of rapid change, the marketplace is governed to a large extent by fundamental natural laws. Studying and understanding these laws gives us a coherent big picture that remains clear even as it changes over time. The picture changes because we go through different growth phases, but it remains clear because the changes conform to laws. Cross-disciplinary approaches offer decision makers long-term dependability and the opportunity to put together winning strategies.

My first book, *Predictions* (see Bibliography), offered a number of insights to help chief executive officers do their jobs better. A person acting as a CEO is already successful, if only because he or she has arrived at that position. My approach consists of helping successful executives become better. Strategic management has been overshadowed by a cloud of confusion. Companies may look good on paper (profitable, on budget, and with great balance sheets) and yet suddenly stumble upon a strategic catastrophe and unexpectedly collapse. Business goes through seasons, and so do the best fit-for-survival strategic initiatives. Large corporations like IBM and Digital Equipment Corporation (DEC) relied on permanence and constant growth. Their successes turned out to be transient and to have well-defined life cycles and time frames.

Management consultants are addressing this transience with increasing fervor. Charles Handy advocates uninterrupted vigilance for the turning point. The beginning of the downturn, he warns, should be assumed imminent at all times, because "there is no science for this sort of thing."[3] But the idea of stubbornly and continuously preparing for a catastrophe is an insult to human intelligence. Common sense tells us it is inefficient to gear continuously for disaster, just as it is dangerous to assume that the good days will last forever. I offer a science in this book that will anticipate the next turning point with *sufficient* accuracy for *just-in-time* action.

Another champion of the transience of success is Adrian Slywotzky—vice president of CDI, an international strategy consulting firm—who demonstrates the transitory aspect of corporations' market value in his book *Value Migration*. He considers only three phases of value movement, however: inflow, stability, and outflow. He ignores the most important business season, "winter," the evolutionary state after growth declines and before it picks up again. In Chap. 2 we will see that the winter season is significant because it allows new directions to be set.

There is more. In both *The Second Curve* by Ian Morrison and *Mission Possible* by Ken Blanchard and Terry Waghorn, the S-shaped sigmoid curve guides decision making through the inevitable decline of one growth phase and the rise of the next one. These authors' treatment, like those of others before them, is qualitative and subjective. The S-shaped pattern, and the reference points on it, are not defined in a rigorous, systematic way.

But the ubiquitous S-shaped curve that enters extensively into everyday life reflects a natural law. It can be used quantitatively to unearth predictability and far-reaching insights. In 1985 DEC saved millions by correctly forecasting the service revenue still due from an old product (see Life Cycles of

Services in Chap. 5). And the British government could have avoided the embarrassment of trying to close down two-thirds of its coal mining pits in 1992 (see Decision Non-Makers in Chap. 7).

The celebrated BCG matrix of the Boston Consulting Group was among the first decision-making tools to divide the life cycle and product portfolio management into four phases. The BCG matrix has been generalized here to handle services, technologies, markets, and anything that grows in competition. Moreover, the approach has now become prescriptive; that is, once strengths and weaknesses have been identified, it estimates the growth potential of each one of them as well as the most appropriate strategy.

Business schools and economics departments in universities around the world produce large amounts of literature on theories, models, guidelines, and strategic advice. Corporations have also become involved in the construction of decision-making tools. One of the difficulties with scenario-planning techniques is that their usefulness varies over time. They are better suited for turbulent low-growth periods, when there are many possible alternatives for action. During an orderly high-growth business season, these techniques offer little help. For example, the multiple-scenario planning methodology of Shell intrigued many but helped few high-level executives. More embarrassing, academic research in general has been of little practical use.

ACADEMIC TOO OFTEN MEANS USELESS

There is a widening gap between academia and the real world. Acquisition of knowledge in academic institutions has, as a rule, no immediate impact on our everyday lives. This fact is openly admitted in such "exotic" places as particle accelerators and other physics laboratories; it is less accepted in departments of softer sciences like biology, anthropology, history, sociology, and psychology. But the gap between research and utility in economics, operations research, and business administration is growing alarmingly. Businesspeople cling to their instinct when it comes to making decisions, and economic forecasts have a dismal track record. Yet millions of dollars are being spent on machinery and human talent for decision-making tools, econometric forecasting models, and business-training activities.

Members of the International Institute of Forecasters and other academic experts regularly debate the widening gap between model building and model using.[4] The volume of publications in economics departments around the country swells, but the benefits to business come in diminishing trickles and only in the long run if at all. Production of knowledge increases exponentially. Each publication triggers more publications. But the public's assimilation can be linear at best. You may learn something new every day, but you could not possibly learn each day more than you learned the day before. Consequently the gap constantly increases. Will this gap eventually reach critical dimensions?

Jay Forrester considers the contrast between great advances in understanding technology and the relative lack of progress in understanding economic and management systems. "Why such a difference?" he asks. "Why has technology advanced so rapidly while social systems continue to exhibit the same kind of misbehavior decade after decade?" His answer lies with the failure to recognize that countries and corporations are indeed *systems*. He has devoted a major part of his life work to *system dynamics*, the study of social systems. A social system implies sources of behavior beyond that of the individual people comprising it. Something about the structure of a system determines what happens other than just the sum of individual objectives and actions. In other words, the concept of a system implies that people are not entirely free agents, but are substantially responsive to their surroundings.[5]

GROWTH DYNAMICS

At Growth Dynamics, an organization founded in 1994 and devoted to strategic forecasting and management consulting, we also employ a cross-discipline systemic viewpoint. We focus on how growth and competition evolve over time, and what leaders can or cannot do. Good professional work is predictable but not predetermined. A concert pianist can and yet does not hit the wrong keys. Enlarging the concept of competition gives us a fascinating big picture. For example, the various forms of transportation compete for passengers, primary energy sources compete for consumers, diseases compete for victims, and words compete for the attention of infants learning how to speak. Some of the results could be far-reaching; for instance, it turns out that natural gas is playing a progressively more important role and will become the dominant primary energy source by 2020. For some high-level executives, results like these may trigger *personal* rather than *industry* decisions (that is, determine the right time to abandon a boat that will sink rather than try to save the boat).

Our aim at Growth Dynamics has been to shed new light on old business problems and to do so in an objective, quantitative way. Objectivity is ensured via the analysis of data and use of the scientific method. Validity is ensured by sticking to a few simple and proven fundamental natural laws that blend harmoniously to present a unified picture. Unlike the academic approach—that is, elaborating complicated formulations to such an extent that they are no longer generally applicable—whenever confronted with an exception, we try to understand it, rather than tamper with the principles. The breadth of the validity of a natural law is proportional to its simplicity.

We have built a number of computer-based interactive tools to assist CEOs and other high-level managers. This book describes in general terms what these tools do, and discusses some historical, nonpersonal case studies. There is roughly a tool behind every chapter.

But the book is meant to offer businesspeople ways of thinking that yield *immediate* value in a variety of everyday situations. Tools and data are not necessary at this point. Even though the approach is rigorous and often quantitative, you will be able to benefit from this book without having to crunch numbers. For example, Chap. 7 guides you through simple steps that will maximize your chances for gaining a second lease on life.

The generalized approach yields guidelines concerning *any* decision. It requires determining the position in the evolutionary cycle you happen to be in and acting *in harmony* with that position. A simplified version is the following two-step approach for quick feedback:

1. Answer the questionnaire in Chap. 2 to establish what "season" you are in concerning a particular issue of interest (such as a competitive growth process).

2. Look up in "The Four Seasons of a Business Cycle" (Chap. 2) the recommendations appropriate for your season and adapt them to the issue in question.

THE S-SHAPED ADVENTURE

- Growth will inevitably decline.
- When exactly is the best time to launch a replacement?
- The revenue dip during product substitution is inevitable but also *desirable*.

In 1984 I abruptly abandoned my academic career to pursue one in industry. I left behind 15 years of research in elementary particle physics to work as a management science consultant for DEC. My boss in the new job, a former physicist himself, tried to smooth the transition by showing me some articles by Cesare Marchetti—a physicist at IIASA in Austria[1]—describing forecasting techniques based on laws from the natural sciences. "See how we are also intellectually alert in industry" was the message. I read the papers with growing enthusiasm. However, 3 weeks later, and in spite of my enthusiasm, the stern new message was "Now leave all this aside and let's get down to work." It was too late, because the subject had intrigued me.

A few months later, I was asked to forecast the life cycles of computer products and the rate at which recent models substitute for older ones. Like Marchetti, I had become a physicist in the business of predicting the future. My reaction was immediate. As soon as I was charged officially with the forecasting project, I took the first plane for Vienna to see Marchetti. My discussions with him proved both exciting and disturbing. On the one hand, his approach appealed to me. The scientific method and the use of biological models such as natural growth and Darwinian competition inspired confidence. On the other hand, there was suspicion; I did not know how much I could trust Marchetti's models. I had to prove to myself that human products indeed fill their market niche the way species fill their ecological niche—that there are laws common to business and biology.

On the return flight I felt a euphoric impatience. I took out my notebook to organize my thoughts and jot down impressions, conclusions, and action plans. I decided to go straight to my office when I arrived late Friday night. I had to try Marchetti's substitution model on the replacement of computers. Marchetti had said that looking at the whole computer market would reveal the detailed competition among the various models. Could this approach describe for me the substitution of computers, as well as it described for Marchetti the substitution of energy sources, means of transportation, and so many other replacements he spoke of? Could it be that replacing large computers by smaller ones is a "natural" process that can be quantified and projected far into the future? Would that be a means of forecasting the future of my company? Could the life cycles of organizations be predicted like those of organisms and, if so, with what accuracy?

In a few months most of my friends and acquaintances knew of my preoccupation with using biological and other scientific formulations to probe the future. To my surprise, other people's interest in my work suddenly became genuine. It was no longer the confusion of those who believe themselves intellectually inferior and stand in awe of something they cannot understand. Now it was more like "This is really interesting! Can I make it work for me?" Everyone who knew of my work was intrigued with the possibility that forecasts could become more reliable through the use of natural sciences. A friend who had just begun selling small sailboats wanted to predict the demand for them next summer on Lake Geneva. Another, in the restaurant business, worried about losing customers and was concerned that his cuisine was too specialized and expensive compared with that of his competition. A depressed young woman was anxious to know when her next love affair would be, and a doctor who had had nine kidney stones in 15 years wanted to know if and when there would be an end to this painful procession.

Besides those eager to believe in the discovery of a miraculous future-predicting device, there were the skeptics. They included those who mistrusted successful forecasts as carefully chosen cases among many failures; those who argued that anyone with an ability to forecast the future would not talk about it, but would get rich on it instead; and those who believed that their future could not be predicted by third parties because it lay squarely in their own hands.

For my part, I soon reached a stage of agonizing indecision. On the one hand, Marchetti's approach appealed to me. The scientific method and the use of biological studies on natural growth and competition inspired confidence. On the other hand, I needed to make my own checks and evaluate the size of the expected uncertainties. I also had to watch out for the trap of losing focus by indulging in the mathematics of the problem. But if in the end I confirmed the existence of an increased capability to forecast, how would I accommodate the predeterminism that it implied? Social beliefs in the ability to shape our future clashed with the fascination of discovering that society has its own ways, which can be quantified and projected reliably into the future. The old question of free will would not be easily resolved.

I searched for more and more cases in which social growth processes fit the description of natural and biological ones. I also searched for discrepancies and carried out extensive simulations to understand the failures. I had embarked upon what I came to call my *S-shaped adventure*, and it took me in surprising directions.[2] Along the way I became convinced that the scientific formulations such as those describing natural growth processes offer a wisdom accessible to everyone and that, when applied to social phenomena, these formulations enable us to interpret and understand the past as well as forecast the future. Furthermore, I learned to visualize most social processes through their life cycles without resorting to mathematics. Such a visualization, I found, offered new perspectives on both the past and the future.

What I have learned from my experience with S-shaped curves, or *S-curves*, can be summarized by two realizations. The first is that many phenomena go through a life cycle: birth, growth, maturity, decline, and death. Time frames vary, making some phenomena look like revolutions and others like natural evolutions. The element in common is *how* the change takes place; for example, the slow and steady way things march to an end is not unlike the way they come into existence. The end of a cycle does not mean a return to the beginning, however. The phases of natural growth proceed along S-curves, cascading from one to the next, in a pattern that reinvokes much of the past but leads to a higher level.

My second realization concerns predictability. There is a promise implicit in a process of natural growth, which is guaranteed by nature: The growth cycle will not stop halfway through—no ecological niche in nature was ever left half full under natural conditions. Whenever I come across a fair fraction of a growth process—in nature, society, business, or my private life—I try to visualize the full life cycle. If I have the first half as given, I can predict the future; if I am faced with the second half, I can deduce the past. I have made peace with my arrogance and have grown to accept that a certain amount of predetermination is associated with *natural* processes, as if by definition from the word *natural*. It is natural, for example, that you do not have the option of making a sharp turn when driving on the highway at 60 miles an hour. At the same time, there are periods—after growth subsides or before it picks up—when there is much choice. You can choose any direction, when you first get in your car.

I have put all this in a book, *Predictions—Society's Telltale Signature Reveals the Past and Forecasts the Future* (Simon & Schuster, 1992). My goal in writing that book was to share my experience with a wider public by showing, in simple terms, the impact this way of thinking about the past and the future can have on everyday life.

Ever since the publication of *Predictions,* I have indulged in extracting practical benefits from these ideas. I founded my own company, Growth Dynamics, at which we continue the research and build techniques and tools to help management teams set and assess their strategies. The book you are now reading demonstrates that management actions are interrelated through natural laws in a coherent way. Understanding these laws will guide your decision making toward winning strategies.

WHAT DO COMPUTERS AND RABBITS HAVE IN COMMON?

They can multiply. What's more, they do it in just about the same way!

...

If you put a pair of rabbits in a meadow, you can watch their population go through an exponential growth pattern at first. As with every multiplication process, one unit brings forth another. But the population growth slows down later as it approaches a ceiling—the capacity of a species' ecological niche. Over time, the rabbit population traces an S-shaped trajectory. The *rate* of growth traces a bell-shaped curve that peaks when half the niche is filled. The S-shaped curve for the population and the bell-shaped curve for its rate of growth constitute a pictorial representation of the natural growth process—that is, how a species population grows into a limited space by obeying the law of survival.

A product's sales follow the same pattern as the product fills its market niche, because competition in the marketplace is intrinsically the same as in the jungle. In my early years with DEC I became involved in describing computer sales with S-shaped curves. The first computer model I tried, one of DEC's early successful minicomputers—the VAX 11/750—illustrated the point. The cumulative number of units sold is shown at the top of Fig. 1-1. The lower graph shows the product's life cycle, the number of units sold each quarter.[3]

When I produced this graph in 1985, I concluded that the product was phasing out, something that DEC's marketers denied vehemently at that time. They refused to accept the conclusions of a physicist. They told me of plans to advertise, drop the price, and repackage the product in order to boost sales. They also spoke of seasonal effects, which would explain the recent low sales.

Sales during the following 3 years turned out to be in line with my predictions. To me, this proved that seasonality, promotional activities, and price changes were conditions present throughout a product's life cycle and would not change the course of a natural phasing-out process estab-

A SUCCESSFUL COMPUTER PRODUCT MAY FILL ITS NICHE LIKE A SPECIES.

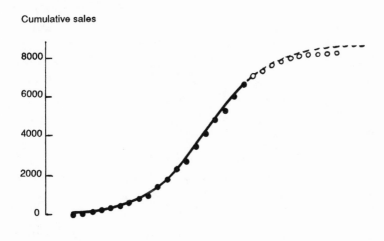

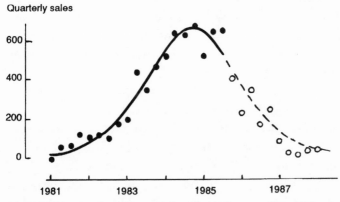

FIGURE 1-1. At the top, growth of cumulative sales in Europe for DEC's minicomputer VAX 11/750. The S-curve is a fit carried out in 1985. The dotted line was my forecast at the time; the open circles show the subsequent sales. The product's life cycle at the bottom has been calculated from the figure at the top.

lished *in the presence* of these conditions. Moreover, the VAX 11/750 was a long-lived, well-positioned product that had its own market niche. Consequently, it faced little competition from other products. The after-the-fact explanation by DEC's marketers that the launching of MicroVAX II (which offered comparable performance for one-third the price) killed the 11/750 in a cannibalization process is an intuitive and inaccurate argument. MicroVAX II was announced three quarters later. It started selling significantly only a year after this forecast spelled out the fate of the 11/750.

Since that time, I have tried to fit S-curves to many products. Often I have been disappointed, particularly when computer models began appearing in rapid succession with little differentiation. Models overlapped and shared market niches with other products. Life cycles became too short and behaved too irregularly to be fitted to a single theoretical curve. What emerged as a better candidate for a growth pattern was a whole family of models, a generation of technology. If I still wanted to study individual products, I would have to take into account the detailed interaction among different models (see Chap. 6).

It has often been noted that inanimate populations do indeed grow along S-curves. There are similarities between the growth of rabbits in a meadow and of automobiles in society. In both cases, growth is capped by a limited resource that becomes scarce as the population competes for it. For rabbits it is grass; for cars it may be space, which is becoming increasingly precious in city centers and on highways.

During the early phases of a rabbit population, the growth is rapid—exponential in mathematical terms. If each pair has two offspring, the population doubles every mating cycle. The element of rapid, exponential-like growth during the early stages is also observable in car populations. In an affluent society one car brings on another. In a household in which both parents have a car, the daughter asks for hers as soon as the son gets his. The number of cars owned by the neighbors may play a role, and it is not unusual for people to own several cars to match various personal needs. The more we become accustomed to cars, the more we need them—at least it seemed that way some time ago.

The conceptual similarity between the way rabbits colonize a field and automobiles "colonize" society points to a common underlying law. The difference lies in the time frame. It may take rabbits months or years to fill up their ecological niche, while it takes cars decades to fill up their "niche" in society. Confirmation of this hypothesis, however, can come only from the real data.

Figure 1-2 plots the data on the annual number of cars officially registered in Italy since 1955.[4] They grow along an

POPULATIONS OF CARS GROW LIKE THOSE OF RABBITS

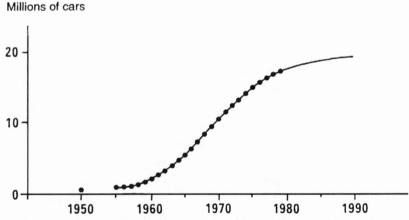

FIGURE 1-2.   Data points and fitted S-curve for the number of registered cars in Italy.

S-curve like rabbits. Because of the large sample of cars, the statistical fluctuations are small and the agreement between the data points and the curve is striking. It is remarkable that world-shaking events like the two oil crises—one in 1974 and the other in 1979—left no mark on the smooth pattern of the growing number of cars, vehicles intimately linked to the availability of oil and the general state of the economy. Many indicators, including oil prices, flared up and subsided during this time period. The oil crises affected car production but not the number of cars in use. During difficult times, people defer buying new cars to save money in the short term. They simply hold on to their old cars longer. The number of cars in use keeps growing in the normal pattern. This number is dictated by a fundamental social need and is not affected by the economic and political climate. In this light, events that produce big headlines may shake the world, but they do not influence the pattern of growth of the number of cars on the street.

Whether it is rabbits in a fenced-off field or automobiles in a free society, there is a progressive substitution of a limited resource by a resident population. If the multiplication is exponential, the overall pattern of growth is symmetric. It is this symmetry that endows S-curves with predictive power: When you are halfway through the process, you know what the other half will be.

It is a remarkably simple and fundamental law. It has been used by biologists to describe the growth under competition of species populations as well as by epidemiologists to describe the diffusion of epidemic diseases. In 1971 J. C. Fisher and R. H. Pry at General Electric published an article that used this law, referred to as the *diffusion model,* to quantify the spreading of new technologies into society. It became a classic in studies of the diffusion of technological change.[5] It is clear how this law applies to abstract concepts as well. Whether it is an idea, a rumor, a technology, or a disease, the rate of new occurrences will always be proportional to how many people already have it and to how many people don't yet have it. This mechanism lies at the heart of competitive growth.

Industrial applications of the S-shaped growth pattern were documented by A. J. Lotka—a physicist at Johns Hopkins University—as early as the turn of the century.[6] More recently, R. Foster at McKinsey & Co. devoted one-third of his book *Innovation: The Attacker's Advantage* to "The S-Curve Method of Business Success."[7] Charles Handy in *The Age of Paradox* exploits "the sigmoid curve" to coach managers on how to avoid premature death.[8] K. Blanchard and T. Waghorn develop Handy's discussion further in their book *Mission Possible*.[9] In my book *Predictions*, I present tens of business applications and many more wider-scope case studies of how the ubiquitous S-curve enters into everyday life.

A species population may begin growing into an ecological niche that is already filled to capacity. In this case the new population can grow only to the extent that another one decreases. Thus a process of *substitution* occurs, and under conditions of natural competition, the transition from occupancy by the old to occupancy by the new should follow the S-shaped pattern. A classical example is the substitution of cars for horses at the beginning of this century.

Figure 1-3 shows the market-share transfer from an old technology to a new one.[10] The regularity of the transition is remarkable, considering that the overall market increased many times during this period and that a world war took place "quietly" in the background. The Darwinian character of the competition becomes visible only when we look at the *relative* position (market share). The advantage of market share is its deeply rooted competitive origin. One competi-

THE SUBSTITUTION OF CARS FOR HORSES IN PERSONAL TRANSPORTATION

As a percentage
of all "vehicles"

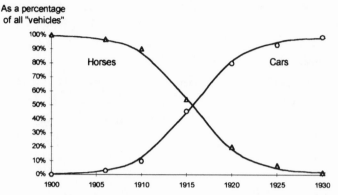

FIGURE 1-3. The data points represent percentages of the total number of transportation units—namely, cars—plus nonfarming horses and mules. The S-curves are fitted to the data points.

tor's gains bear directly on another competitor's losses. The description thus becomes free of external influences: economy, politics, earthquakes, and seasonal effects such as vacations and holidays.

A substitution—between products, services, technologies, or simply ways of doing things—is *natural* to the extent that it evolves along an S-shaped pattern. One-to-one replacements do that. For some substitutions, however, identifying a natural character is not so obvious and may require more than just looking at the usual market shares. This was the case with the split of Arthur Andersen into accounting and consulting divisions, and the loss of market value by IBM and DEC in favor of Microsoft and Intel.

In 1989 Arthur Andersen split into two independent units, one for accounting and one for consulting. The move was a response to the growth of the firm's consulting practice during the early 1980s and the problems that growth posed for profit sharing, status in the company, customer image, and strategy. The incremental growth of the consulting practice amounted to one-fourth of the firm's total revenue. The detailed transfer from the hands of the accountants to the hands of the consultants was a natural process that began in the early 1980s and was completed in the mid-1990s. When the belated split took place in 1989, the process was already 64 percent complete.

Another example of a not-obvious natural replacement is the loss of market value by IBM and DEC in favor of Microsoft and Intel. One way to measure a company's market value is by its capitalization (shares outstanding times stock price, plus long-term debt). Adrian Slywotzky has reported that during the last 10 years IBM and DEC lost tens of billions in market value to Microsoft and Intel.[11]

The percentages of combined market value in Fig. 1-4 show that the change of hands took place in a natural way.[12] It is natural because the trajectories are S-shaped. Because it is natural, it is predictable. Figure 1-4 tells us that this mar-

TRANSFER OF MARKET VALUE

As a percentage of the
combined market value

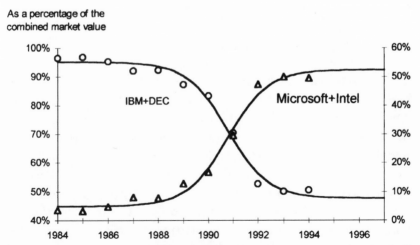

FIGURE 1-4. In 10 years Microsoft and Intel took half the market value held by IBM and DEC. The S-curves are fits to the data points.

TRANSFER OF REVENUE SHARE IN ARTHUR ANDERSEN

As a percentage
of all revenue

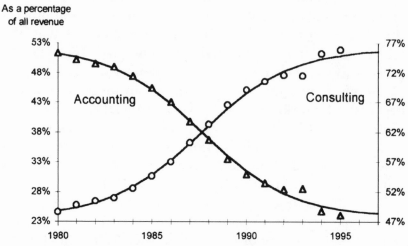

FIGURE 1-5. During the last 15 years, one-fourth of the revenue in Arthur Andersen changed hands from accounting to consulting. The data come from annual company reports. The S-curves are fits to the data points.

ket value transfer was a well-established, accurately predictable process by 1991. Similarly, Fig. 1-5 suggests that the split of Arthur Andersen should have happened—and could have been predicted—at least a couple of years earlier.[12]

The natural character of substitutions is not visible if we look at the absolute numbers, which is what annual reports and journalists usually highlight. The S-curves of Fig. 1-3— the cars-for-horses substitution—are not visible in Fig. 1-6, which reflects mostly the explosive growth of this market.[13] Something else is now visible. Despite the pronounced upward trend, a dip occurs in the overall market trend during the transition years. Such a dip is familiar to marketers concerned with product substitutions and to experienced strategic planners concerned with technology or other major substitutions.

THE OVERALL PERSONAL "VEHICLE" MARKET

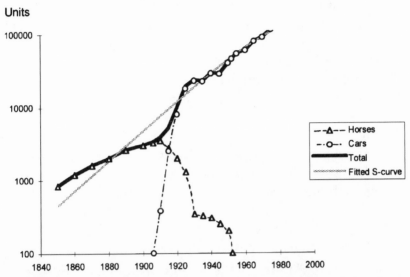

FIGURE 1-6. The number of nonfarming horses (including mules) and cars in the United States. The vertical scale is logarithmic to accommodate the explosive growth. The fitted line is an S-curve. Despite impressive growth, the sum of horses plus cars suffered during the substitution years.

Wishful marketers set out to minimize the low-growth period and, if possible, eliminate it—for example, by having the growth steps so close together that the overall growth rate remains practically constant. But it is naive to attribute the dip to retarded product announcements. Launching the new product long before the old one becomes exhausted will surely result in "cannibalism" (undercutting your own market), as was thought to be the case with DEC's mini-computers VAX 11/750 and MicroVAX II mentioned earlier. However, it is also naive to believe that a phasing-out product can be revived by repackaging, advertising, price cutting, and the like. A hard fact of life is that a well-established phasing-out process runs a natural exiting course, one that may be self-defeating to fight. Things are different when we move from one-to-one substitution to competition among several products (or processes) for the same market niche. In this case advertising and pricing can indeed be effective (see Chap. 6).

A uniformly constant growth rate is unrealistic because it does not represent a natural process. There is no "secret of constant growth," as Charles Handy pretends in his discussion of the sigmoid curve in *The Age of Paradox*. On the contrary, the dip in revenue is not simply natural and inevitable. It is desirable. The dip plays a significant role in triggering new growth, just as pruning the roses ensures healthier blossoms for the next season. We will examine closely the merits of low-growth business seasons in Chap. 2. The important point here is that business executives facing a major transition between products, technologies, or other processes should plan for and anticipate a low-growth period comparable in duration—as we'll see in the next section—to the high-growth period they just enjoyed. The marketer's only compensatory action is the classical product portfolio approach of the Boston Consulting Group. BCG advocates holding a variety of products, not all of which would be in the precarious transitional phase simultaneously.

JUST-IN-TIME INNOVATION

Successful product substitution does not mean ever-increasing revenues. Any substitution means that the overall growth rate will drop before it rises again. The natural growth processes, shown by S-curves at the top of Fig. 1-7, cascade in a *harmonic* way.[15] The word *harmonic* is used rigorously here. It means that the processes cascade in such

NATURAL GROWTH *HARMONIOUSLY* SUSTAINED

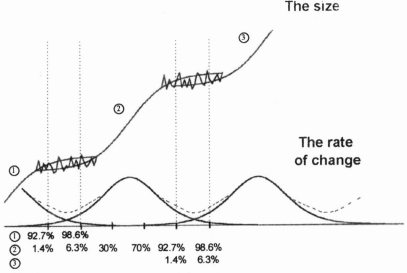

①	92.7%	98.6%				
②	1.4%	6.3%	30%	70%	92.7%	98.6%
③					1.4%	6.3%

FIGURE 1-7. Harmonic succession of natural growth processes means a pendulum swing from one market niche to the next, while survival of the fittest dictates the rule of competition. The graph at the top shows the amount of growth achieved during the consecutive filling of three market niches. The graph at the bottom shows the rate of growth. The percentages refer to the niche penetration level. The overall rate of growth (dotted line at the bottom) indicates a cyclical sine-wave pattern. During low-growth periods chaotic oscillations become evident.

a way that the overall envelope (shown in the lower graph of Fig. 1-7) traces a sine wave, the hallmark of harmonic motion.[14] That is the way a pendulum moves. The implication is that the new product must have penetrated its market niche by 1 percent when the old product approaches filling its own market niche to 90 percent. This is *just-in-time* product replacement. It ensures that when the old product reaches the end of its life cycle (99 percent of total sales), the new product has come out of "infant mortality" with 7 percent penetration of its own market niche and can thus assume the main thrust of the new growth phase. On the time axis of Fig. 1-7 we see precisely how the market penetration levels overlap.

Just-in-time replacement is based on the intellectually appealing hypothesis that *harmony* should be associated with sustained *natural* growth. There is hard evidence that corroborates this hypothesis, however. Market-niche succession—documented by data—has followed this rule on at least two occasions: in energy consumption worldwide, discussed in Chap. 2, and in the evolution of coal production in the United States over the last 150 years, reported in *Predictions.*[15] Both cases depict a pattern identical to that of Fig. 1-7.

The overall drop associated with the period of transition becomes more pronounced if the product substitution coincides with the appearance of new technologies. The first RISC (reduced instruction set computing) computers sold poorly when they were introduced, as did the first 64-bit processors. In both cases, the easy explanation was the lack of adequate software applications that would run on these new platforms. As true as this may be, it also reflects the *natural* difficulties associated with a major change. But on a more macroscopic and philosophical level, there are deeper-seated reasons for the dip. It constitutes a low-growth business season, thus giving rise to a cyclical variation. As the pendulum moves, it alternates between two states: one of purely potential energy and another of purely kinetic energy—a state of potential growth and a state of visible growth. Such periodic change has proved beneficial climatically, culturally, and socially. We will see in the next chapter that diversity is also beneficial to business.

STRUCTURING AN ENTERPRISE ACCORDING TO ITS SEASON

- "If winter is here, can spring be far behind?"
  Percy B. Shelley
- Where am I (my products, my business units, or my company) on the curve?
- How should my way of making decisions evolve as I move across the life cycle?

Business, like the weather, goes through seasons, and so do the correct management policies. Is your company appropriately "dressed" for the season it is entering? Products, companies, and entire industries experience the same weatherlike fluctuations as agricultural crops. At the same time, they go through seasons in a cyclical way. Summer is the high-growth period around the midpoint of the cycle. Winters are the low-growth periods at the end and at the beginning of the process. Between winter and summer comes spring, characterized by a progressively rising growth rate. Fall is the time between summer and winter, when the rate of growth continuously declines.

On a large time scale, the 1990s represent a season of winter for the coal industry worldwide, despite the popular uprising that followed the British government's decision to close down more than 60 percent of the country's mining pits in late 1992. In contrast, the mobile electronics industry (for example, cellular phones and portable computers) is enjoying exponential growth trends characteristic of a spring season. Consulting and software firms find themselves in summer, when the living is easy and the profits are high. Microsoft's hefty earnings exceed expectations, Electronic Data Systems (EDS) posts record earnings, and Arthur Andersen partners indulge in gala annual meetings with record-breaking attendance. Traditional computer hardware manufacturers from the biggest (IBM, DEC, Unisys) to the less big (Cray, Tandy, Commodore) are tightening their belts for a winter that promises growth rates close to or below zero. At the same time, new industries organized around knowledge bases, the Internet, and the environment are approaching spring, with buds ready to blossom.

Borrowing images from biology to fit the marketplace is not new. Companies resemble living organisms. They are born, mature, get married, have offspring, become aggressive, sleepy, or exhausted, grow old, and eventually die or fall victim to voracious predators. As early as the turn of the century, enlightened economists and broad-minded physicists applied scientific notions such as periodic harmonic motion and Darwin's survival of the fittest to human products. In 1918 Lotka successfully predicted the size of the completed American railway network, via mathematical formulations from biology.[1] At about the same time (1926), the Russian economist Nikolai D. Kondratieff was establishing evidence for a long economic wave of 50 to 60 years. This claim scored high points in popularity when the stock market crashed in 1987 and continued to score high with the persistent depressionlike economy that, as had happened 58 years earlier, followed the 1987 crash.[2]

Periodic swings of the economy are echoed in the preachings of management consulting gurus, who pass easily from thesis to antithesis and do not stop short of giving contradictory messages. Do you find your company investing in business process reengineering and total quality—zero defects—at the same time? Have you reconciled the benefits of leadership with those of empowerment and self-managed teams? Advocates of centralized control and vertical integration became rather quiet in the 1990s. Instead we heard about business units, core competencies, and horizontal corporations. These changes do not reflect conceptual breakthroughs in the theory of doing business. They are simply reactions to the economic climate and its seasonal variation.

Throughout history, periods of bureaucracy and control have been interspersed by waves of innovation and entrepreneurship. Notorious bureaucracies, such as the Roman Empire and the British civil service, were preceded and followed by entrepreneurial eras, such as crusades and revolutions (both social and industrial). The way to do business has followed suit. Many have addressed the question of how organizational behavior evolves over time. But it was Niccolo Machiavelli—early in the sixteenth century—who first pointed out the importance of adaptation. He wrote in *The Prince*: "I believe also that he will be successful who directs his actions according to the spirit of the times, and that he whose actions do not accord with the times will not be successful."

THE FOUR SEASONS OF
A BUSINESS CYCLE

Many management theorists divide the growth cycle—typically a product's sales cycle—into segments. Theorists generally consider four periods according to the phase of growth: start-up, rapid growth, maturation, and decline. Their treatment is invariably qualitative, and the four phases are not necessarily of equal duration or precise definition.

This chapter presents the business cycle somewhat differently, using the four seasons as a metaphor. Here winter reflects the critical growth period encountered during the beginning and the end of a natural growth process. Products experience two winters in their lifetimes. The first winter is while they are struggling for a foothold in the marketplace, and the second one comes when they are exiting and the follow-up product is fighting for succession. By definition, the end of the first winter signals that the growth process has survived "infant mortality"—that is, it has realized around 7 percent of its growth potential.

The seasons metaphor has more than poetic justification. The advantage over more traditional segmentations is that our familiarity with the mechanisms associated with nature's four seasons can shed light on and guide us through decisions on business and social issues. For example, the low creativity observed during summer is only partially due to the heat. New undertakings are disfavored mainly because summer living is easy and there is no reason to look for change. In contrast, animals (for example, foxes and sparrows) are known to become entrepreneurial in winter. There is wisdom encoded in nature's seasonal behavior patterns. These can be studied and transferred to whatever situation depicts a succession of seasonlike stages. It is conceivable to exploit the analogy all the way down to monthly behaviors.

Like the four seasons, the segments into which we divide the cycle must be of equal length. The time scale may vary widely depending on what growth process we are looking at. For a product, a season may last 6 months to a year. For an industry, a season may be 5 to 10 years. For the world economy cycling through 50- to 60-year waves, a season may be 15 years long.

We saw in Chap. 1 that just-in-time product substitution is achieved when 1 percent of the new product's market penetration coincides with 90 percent saturation of the old product's market niche. This timing implies that the replacing product's first winter coincides with the incumbent product's second winter. Consequently the timing also implies that the new product must be launched during the fall season of the product it is replacing (no wonder farmers sow in autumn). Winter then becomes the time of selection, when wanton death eliminates the weak and the unfit. Spring corresponds to adolescence, the formative years. Spring is also the time for R&D of future replacements.

Most product managers have intuitive knowledge of the product-succession sequence. They know, for example, that a new product is promoted most heavily while the old product phases out—to be precise, during the last 12.5 percent of its life cycle, its second winter. They also know that research and development for the new product must parallel capacity buildup for the old product, which is approaching a maximum rate of sales and profitability.

Figure 2-1 defines seasons not only for products but for anything that grows in competition: markets, technologies, industries, and so on.[3] It is generally true that spring is concerned with the *what* and fall with the *how*. That is why at the industry level product innovation occurs in spring and process innovation in fall. At the same time, at the economy level, technology and finances dominate in spring, and social and political forces dominate in fall. Spring is the time for investments. It is also the time for learning and continuous improvement. Specialists are in demand. Not so in winter. Several years ago I explained to a Geneva bank director that winter is the time to fire bureaucrats and to hire Leonardo da Vincis—that is, cross-disciplinary, well-rounded men and women who stand a better chance than specialists to come

ASSIGNING SEASONS TO THE LIFE CYCLE

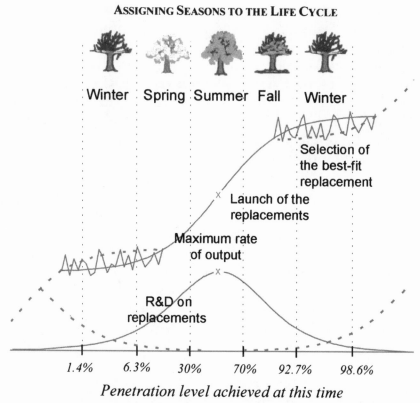

Winter   Spring Summer Fall   Winter

Selection of
the best-fit
replacement

Launch of the
replacements

Maximum rate
of output

R&D on
replacements

1.4%   6.3%   30%   70%   92.7%   98.6%

Penetration level achieved at this time

FIGURE 2-1.   Segmentation of a business cycle into four seasons. The growth levels at the delimiting positions satisfy the following two conditions: (1) all seasons have the same duration, and (2) the early winter of the replacement overlaps with the late winter of the incumbent. Low-growth periods are accompanied by large and chaotic fluctuations.

up with revolutionary ideas for profitable business. "Fire bureaucrats is exactly what we need to do, sir," he exclaimed. "Could you please tell us how to do it?" To my surprise, I heard 2 months later that the man had been fired.

But often what naturally happens is what should happen. As strange as it may sound, seeing your specialists progressively evolve into bureaucrats may be a good sign. It is one indication that summer is setting in. The word *bureaucrats* carries a negative connotation, but if we call them *process agents* instead, we realize that they provide an important function during times of high growth and prosperity. It is during summer that enterprises become successful, centralized, conservative (no one tampers with something that works well), and in need of clockwork operations. Fine-tuning and zero defects (the original aspiration of total quality management) are particularly appropriate for a summer season. But then, what about benchmarking, continuous improvement, and BPR (business process reengineering)?

SECOND THOUGHTS ABOUT EXCELLENCE

Being second best hardly yields a competitive advantage. But positive feedback theories, that produce rapid fluctuations resembling chaos, argue that early gains for two simultaneously launched competitors eventually tilt the balance in favor of the "lucky" one and not necessarily the better one.[4] Early gains do not presuppose excellence.

When videocassette recorders were introduced, the market was split between VHS and Beta. The two market shares fluctuated early on because of circumstances, luck, or marketing tactics. But soon early returns tilted the unstable situation toward VHS despite claims that Beta was technically superior. There are many such examples. Connoisseurs of personal computers value Apple products more highly than IBM computers and their clones, but the market share gains of the latter have biased standardization in their favor.

Such manifestations of positive feedback mechanisms have long been understood. During the last century Alfred Marshall—professor of political economy in Bristol, England—wrote that whatever firm first gets a good start will corner the market. To get a good early start, a product must appeal to the masses rather than to the elite, and that argues for postponing sophistication and refinements for a later season. New products are launched in the fall, but excellence is only excellent in the summer.

It is worth looking in more detail at each season's characteristics and how they can help us with everyday work decisions. There are advantages and disadvantages to each season. As we go through the various characteristics, keep in mind that they are meant to be in *relative* terms—that is, whatever happens in one season is with respect to what happened during the previous seasons. For example, to say that competition is lowest in spring does not mean it is negligible. It simply means that competition is *relatively* lower in spring than during the other seasons.

WINTER

Advantage	*Disadvantage*
New ideas	Low profits

Winter is the beginning and the end. Death comes naturally only in winter. That is why survival becomes the name of the game. People are anxious, confused, and frustrated and explore new directions. During the chaos of winter, profound changes take place. Enterprises focus on core competencies and organize themselves horizontally. Multidisciplinary generalists are in demand. This is the time to fire bureaucrats, train and reskill the rest of the workforce, and mobilize entrepreneurs. Business becomes culture-driven, and enterprises go after niche markets with short-term strategies. Bottom-up cultural forces dominate and lead to segmentation, decentralization, and horizontal markets. Leadership becomes ineffective while empowerment becomes popular.

Winter is the most difficult but also the most fertile season. Despite low morale, innovation and creativity are at a high. New directions are set. It is a period of selection. Mutations come out in great numbers and compete for the next position in power. Most of them will die, but those that make it to springtime will be ensured of a full growth cycle. Mutations serve the purpose of emergency reserves. In industry they can take the form of new product ideas, basic innovations, or other ventures. The higher their number, the better the chance that some of them will survive and grow, paving the way for the sunnier seasons that lie ahead.

The buzzwords of the management consulting gurus that become fashionable during this season are: *change management, self-management, BPR, SBUs (strategic business units)*, and *niche markets*. Economically winter is the period of depression. On the product side:

- Prices become customer-driven and may not yield a profit.
- The salesforce becomes opportunistic.
- Recently launched products face the acid test: Will they live or will they die?

During *early winter*, risk taking is encouraged, and new ways of thinking and ideas for new lines of business abound. *Late winter* is the time to choose among these new directions. It is critical to identify which direction will realize around 7 percent of its growth potential—the hallmark of surviving infant mortality—by the end of winter.

Industrial winters are mutational. At these times industries explore and adapt themselves in order to penetrate the maximum number of new niches. The microprocessor industry, for example, demonstrated during its winter—the first 15 years of its existence, 1970 to 1985—an impressive ability to come up with an ever-increasing number of unexpected uses for chips. In the last 10 years, this industry has come out of winter and is climbing up the exponential growth rates of spring.

	Advantage Disadvantage
Spring	Excitement High investments

In spring, progressive growth and new opportunities bring hope, excitement, and elation. Competition reaches a relative low point as people concentrate on hard-work ethic to enhance prosperity. Spring is a period of learning and continuous improvement. It is also a period of acquisitions and investments in facilities and real estate. Operations can benefit from an attitude of wise wastefulness. Innovation in spring concerns the S-curves of one level below. For example, the spring of an industry means product innovation. The spring of the economy—on a longer time scale—means industry innovation.

On the product side, spring demands the following:

- Build capacity for and ramp up the sales of recently launched products.
- Set prices according to value offered.
- Do R&D on the follow-up products.

The most solicited human resources are specialists, engineers, and designers, men and women who resemble well-hardened and sharpened tools. Leaders are trained in view of the approaching season of prosperity. In the United States today, the pollution abatement "industry" is in its spring. It has gone beyond infant mortality but has not yet reached maturity. Now at a few percentage points of GNP, pollution abatement is estimated to reach a ceiling at around 10 percent. When the whole economy is in spring, inflation is low, the value of money is high, and the recommendation for stocks is *buy.*

Early spring is the time when chaos subsides; opportunism and entrepreneurship lose their luster. *Late spring* is the right time to set up leadership schools, since leaders will abound in the upcoming summer.

SUMMER

Advantage	Disadvantage
High profits	Low creativity

As summer sets in, the enterprise becomes successful, centrally controlled, vision-driven (by top-down unifying forces), and conservative. You do not tamper with something that works well. You are allowed only to fine-tune it. This is the time for excellence and total quality (nine sigmas on the rate of rejects, if you can). Good leadership is in demand and enjoys stability. Process agents—inspectors who check and control processes—are also in demand. Conveniently, many specialists are now naturally evolving into bureaucrats. Strategies become long-term and strategic alliances frequent. A more vertical (stovepipe) organization comes back into fashion.

Output is at a maximum and supplies the S-curves one level below. That is, the summer of a technology sees the largest number of successful products. The summer of the economy—on a longer time scale—sees the largest number of profitable industries. Buzzwords include *vision, excellence, long-range planning,* and *TQM.* On the product side:

- Sell, sell, sell (milk the cow).
- Dictate your prices (decadent profits).
- Integrate vertically.

To expand market share further, you do not hesitate to sell all things to all people. Advertising budgets swell. It is a period of fun and games. But comfort may lead to boredom and decadence.

Early summer is a time to stop investing and concentrate on reaping profits. But pay attention! *Late summer* is the turning point. Cash cows are by now getting old. It is high time to plan for the approaching days of diminishing growth.

U.S. steel companies have enjoyed the longest summer of any industry. For the better part of this century, continuous success made steelmakers conservative and immutable. But in more recent decades, the industry has been shaken by the rising popularity of competitive new materials. By the 1990s most steel industries worldwide were indulging in reorganization and process innovation, a clear sign of losing ground.

FALL

Advantage	Disadvantage
Bearing fruit	Aging

You are probably too familiar with the instinctive human reaction to loss of market share: denial, blame, and panic, in that chronological order. These are the hallmarks of the fall season. The usual rescue efforts include tightening-the-belt programs, face-lifting efforts, and a concentration on core competencies. What is excellent to start with is benchmarking, a comparative study to find out what you are not doing quite right. A back-to-basics attitude makes operations shrink. The company disinvests from aging products and focuses on strategic accounts. On a longer time scale, the fall of an industry sees process innovation. On an even longer time scale, the fall of the economy sees recession, high inflation, and a rush toward liquidity. But deteriorating trends soon enter a state of chaos, in which erratic behavior emerges as a mechanism to explore new directions picked practically at random. Competition intensifies to a maximum. Cross-disciplinary generalists must be recruited to devise revolutionary ideas for profitable new business.

On the product side:

- Set prices according to costs.
- Improve efficiency of operations, particularly on phasing-out products.
- Launch the replacement product.

During *early fall,* sobering up and tightening-the-belt tactics suffice, but as the season matures, cost-cutting and face-lifting operations are no longer effective. *Late fall* is the time to redesign your processes and begin the search for or the training of entrepreneurs. Fall is also the time to teach what you have learned.

Figure 2-2 provides highlights for each season. It is possible to exploit the seasons' characteristics in order to devel-

HIGHLIGHTS OF SEASONAL RECOMMENDATIONS

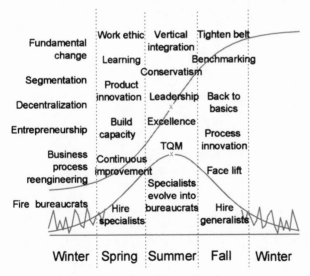

FIGURE 2-2.   General guidelines for what is appropriate in a given season.

op investment strategies. The typical pattern is to invest in spring and go liquid in fall. More detailed guidelines are given below—including, in parentheses, dates for the American investor. In late 1997 I estimated that the U.S. economy was in a late spring, and that the season's duration was at least 7 years long (see Where Are You on the Curve? below). Assuming that the season's duration is indeed 7 years—that is, assuming that inflation would begin rising again in 1998—I made the following recommendations:

- *Spring (1990–1997):* Buy shares; buy commodities; sell gold.
- *Summer (1997–2004):* Sell commodities.
- *Fall (2004–2011):* Sell shares; buy gold.
- *Winter (2011–2018):* Buy bonds; sell gold.

TYPICAL BEHAVIORAL PATTERNS

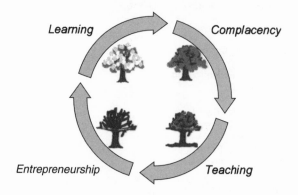

Learning   *Complacency*

Entrepreneurship   *Teaching*

LIKE SHAKESPEAREAN PLAYS

Shakespeare classified plays into four types that can be matched to the four seasons. A coherent picture emerges when we tabulate them with fundamental desires, needs, questions, and roles.

SPRING	SUMMER	FALL	WINTER
Romance	Comedy	Tragedy	Satire
You do not have what you want.	You have what you want.	You have what you do not want.	You do not have what you do not want.
What	Why not	How	Why
Composer	Administrator	Performing artist	Philosopher

This table makes common sense. *Spring* fever is inextricably related to *not having what you want.* (If Dante's love for Beatrice had been consummated, his passion would have fizzled, and he might never have written the *Divine Comedy.*) *Romantic* is probably the most frequently used adjective for a *composer. What* to do is the main preoccupation in the spring phase of any project.

During *summer, you have what you want* (for example, fun and games) and consequently you do not ask questions. The only question you might ask would be *why not* keep doing the same thing? And it so happens that there is indeed something *comic* about *bureaucrats* and *administrators.*

During *fall* you are *tragically* stuck with something *you do not want* (for example, getting old or being trapped in a tired relationship). Your efforts to improve a deteriorating situation make the *how* a more important question than the what, for which there is no longer a choice. Inversely, if you see the emphasis put on the process (for example, process redesign), you can safely surmise that something is getting old. *Tragic* is probably the most significant adjective for the work of a *performing artist.*

Winter is like after the divorce. *You no longer have what you do not want.* You become introspective and may start asking *why. Philosophers* are often *satirical.* But remember,

OPERATIONS

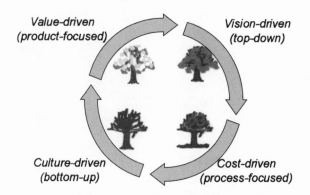

Value-driven
(product-focused)

Vision-driven
(top-down)

Culture-driven
(bottom-up)

Cost-driven
(process-focused)

WHAT BEST CHARACTERIZES THE ENVIRONMENT

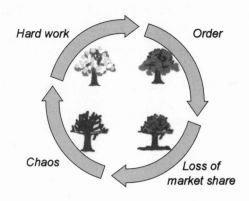

Hard work

Order

Chaos

Loss of
market share

winter is not only the time when the old dies; it is also in winter that the new is conceived.

In addition to the above descriptions, we should consider two more remarks that offer a general insight (or warning) about the four seasons. Summer and winter tend to be dry and physical but are characterized by lucidity. Spring and fall are more humid and emotional, and consequently more illusionary.

THE BCG MATRIX REVISITED

The Boston Consulting Group, founded in 1963 by Bruce Henderson, has become known for its growth-share matrix, a diagram of the normal relationship between cash use and cash generation. The concept behind the BCG matrix is something Henderson first came across with the U.S. defense industry and later applied to electronics. Namely, the more airplanes that were built, the less time each unit took, and therefore the cheaper they became to produce. This is a formulation of the economies of scale—the industry curve. The Boston Consulting Group derived a portfolio management picture positioning products in four quadrants according to two variables: market growth and market share.[5] The quadrants were labeled as follows:

- *Stars* occupied the high-growth high-share quadrant.
- *Cash cows* occupied the low-growth high-share quadrant.
- *Dogs* occupied the low-growth low-share quadrant.
- *Question marks* occupied the high-growth low-share quadrant.

Looking at the description of each quadrant and what usually happens to products, we realize that the BCG matrix supplies a well-defined direction for the evolution of things. *Stars* become *cash cows*, which become *dogs*, and when they become bigger *dogs* they effectively are *question marks*, some of which may become *stars*. This cyclical movement is driven by changes in growth and market share.

The labeling of each quadrant of the BCG matrix reflects the combination of market growth and product growth. For example, *cash cows*, despite their high rate of sales, are associated with a low-growth period of the market.

At Growth Dynamics we have developed a new, more general, and self-contained version of the BCG matrix. This version handles the evolution over time of *any* business entity that grows in competition: products, services, technologies, markets, organizations, SBUs, departments, functions, processes, and the like. Our variables are somewhat different. Instead of market share, we look at the actual degree of satisfaction, and instead of market growth, we consider the amount of future interest expected. But the most important difference is that our definition of the four segments—the seasons—refers only to the entity's rate of growth across its life cycle.

In our matrix (see Fig. 2-3), *opportunities*—spring—refer

THE BCG MATRIX AS MODIFIED BY GROWTH DYNAMICS

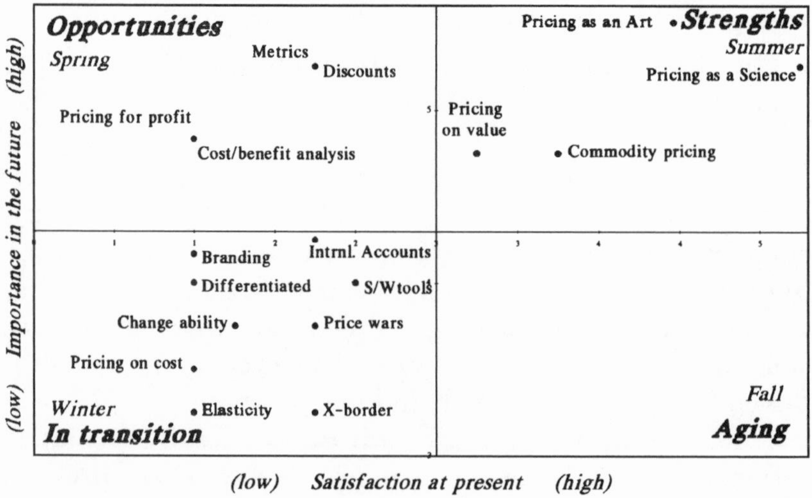

FIGURE 2-3.   The data represent the answers given by the pricing managers participating at the Eighth Annual Pricing Conference in Chicago in April 1995.

to entities in a phase of early growth; opportunities correspond to *stars*. *Strengths*—summer—refer to entities in a high-growth period; strengths correspond to *cash cows*. *Aging*—fall—refers to whatever undergoes declining growth and corresponds to a *dog*. *In transition*—winter—refers to entities with very low growth; they correspond to *question marks*. The advantage of defining things this way is that now we can use the decision support machinery of the seasons discussed earlier.

One interactive software tool developed at Growth Dynamics is a quick-feedback questionnaire that produces results online. The technique has been used with such firms as Baxter International (health and medical products) and HLB International (accounting firms) as well as in a number of business conferences. Figure 2-3 shows an example of results obtained during the Eighth Annual Pricing Conference in Chicago in April 1995.

One of our findings was that pricing managers treat pricing not only as an art but also as a science. This dual view indicates that there is no perceived clear-cut advantage of an instinctive versus an analytical approach to pricing, something we will examine in more depth in Chap. 5. Still, pricing as an art came out more important for the future but less under control at present.

Other highlights based on the perception of pricing managers at the April 1995 Chicago conference follow:

- Price wars were found in a winter season as if they were tactics of low value (*dogs* in the classical BCG matrix).
- Similarly—but to a lesser extent—the use of software tools for setting prices was also found in a winter.
- Pricing according to value was found in a summer (a *strength*).

One should expect such results to change with time,

however. It is not excluded that price wars and software pricing tools become *opportunities* some time in the future.

We estimated the length of the business season for a few of the entries in our matrix. The audience's pricing practices were found to be in good agreement with the seasonal interpretation of correct business decisions. If we consider the U.S. economy in early 1995 as being in a spring, pricing for value should be the predominant practice, whereas pricing for profit would be considered more appropriate for the next season. Accordingly, Fig. 2-3 shows pricing for profit in the spring quadrant, since most managers considered it to be an opportunity for the future.

The original BCG matrix has been criticized as too simplistic. Its author, Bruce Henderson, explained that the BCG matrix was never meant to be prescriptive but was intended only as an innovative way to describe a business. In the modified version discussed above, the Growth Dynamics graphs can become prescriptive strategy-planning tools. By positioning many processes (or products) in their business seasons, we can develop guidelines about what to do according to the seasonal recommendations given earlier. Furthermore, the analysis can be enhanced in two ways. First, we can now determine more accurately—quantitatively—a product's position in the season and the season's length. Second, we can determine the remaining growth potential for each one of the entries in the BCG matrix. Both enhancements can be achieved using such interactive software as Growth Dynamics' *Power of Strategic Evolution*.[6]

WHERE ARE YOU ON THE CURVE?

Oedipus became king of Thebes, according to the ancient Greek tragedy, by resolving the longstanding riddle "Which unique being walks at times on two, at times on three, at times on four legs, and is weaker the more legs he walks on?" (see Fig. 2-4.)

You can build winning strategies by answering a somewhat related question: "Where are you on the curve?" The time frame can vary. If it is decades, you are probably addressing your whole life, or your company's existence from beginning to end. If it is years or months, you may be concerned with a product's life cycle, or a business season, and there will be many seasons before your company or technology ceases to exist.

In Chap. 5 you will find techniques for quantitatively estimating your position on the curve. Here you can rely on a simple but powerful intuitive approach for determining the cycle phase you are in. It is based on the fact that

WHERE ARE YOU ON THE CURVE?

FIGURE 2-4. A visual representation of the riddle that the Sphinx put to Oedipus.

the *prospects for growth* affect your emotional disposition—subconsciously—and thus become intuitively accessible.

The method utilizes the concepts of calculus. The S-shaped overall pattern is very sensitive to the rate of change of the rate of growth. Mathematically, this corresponds to the second derivative—in other words, the prospects for growth. To better understand the concept of the second derivative, think of traveling in your car. Let us say that the *distance* you cover as a function of time looks like an S-shaped curve. (This does not mean that you swerve around but that you change speeds as you drive.) The first derivative—the rate at which the distance changes—is the car *speed.* When the speed is high, much distance is covered in a short time. The speed curve is typically bell-shaped—that is, low in the beginning and at the end, but high in the middle of the trip. The second derivative is the *acceleration,* the rate at which the speed changes. The acceleration is directly proportional to the force exerted by the car. The more powerful the car, the higher a speed it can attain in a short time. This curve goes up and down and up again, since you start at zero, accelerate, and then decelerate in order to stop. Figure 2-5 shows the three curves mathematically calculated. Without loss of generality, the second derivative has been approximated with straight-line segments to conform to the seasons.

A more relevant example is found in product sales. As we saw, the cumulative number of products sold—the filling of the market niche—is described by an S-shaped curve. Sales *per quarter* represent the first derivative. They comprise the product's life cycle and follow a bell-shaped curve. In this case, the second derivative is the company's *investment* in its product. Investment is positive during the prod-

DIFFERENT WAYS OF LOOKING AT NATURAL GROWTH

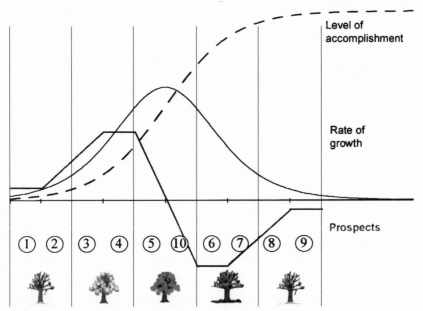

FIGURE 2-5. Three curves describing a natural growth process: the S-curve and its two derivatives (the second derivative has been approximated with straight-line segments). The circled numbers correspond to the numbers of the questionnaire; they point out a position in a season.

uct's early days and negative—returns instead of investment—during the product's later life.

Similarly, in the stock market, the share price during a growth cycle is described by an S-shaped curve. The returns on investment per unit of time are given by the bell-shaped curve. The second derivative reflects the prospects for growth, something like the analysts' ratings of A+, A, A−, or three stars, two stars, and so on.

For *any* growth process, we need to identify the quantity that corresponds to its second derivative—that is, *the rate of the rate* of growth, or the prospects for growth. Here are some examples:

S-SHAPED CURVE	BELL-SHAPED CURVE (FIRST DERIVATIVE)	UP AND DOWN AND UP (SECOND DERIVATIVE)
Distance	Speed	Acceleration (force)
Cumulative sales of product	Sales by quarter	Investments in product
Size of organism	Rate of growth	Growth prospects
Stock price	ROI	Stock rating
Knowledge	Learning	Rate of progress
State of economy (GNP, $ per capita, etc.)	Rate of economic development	Value of money (opposite of inflation)

You can pinpoint your position in the growth cycle by answering a questionnaire that addresses your emotional world. The questionnaire determines your position in the cycle with an accuracy of half a season. As you respond, think of the prospects for the future and the direction in which they are moving. Or simply whether you feel good or bad, optimistic or pessimistic toward the future—all with regard to a product, an activity, a company, a career, or whatever else may be on your mind. But remember, the activity you choose must grow under conditions of natural competition—that is, the law of survival of the fittest.

When employees or stockholders complete such a questionnaire on their company as a whole, they reveal more than their perception and mood. They give a better determination of the company's position in the business cycle than the opinions of its management team. Let us try answering the questionnaire together.

What Are the Prospects for the Future?
(Check one box.)

POSITIVE	NEGATIVE
1-☐ Very low and stable	Very negative and stable 6-☐
2-☐ Low and rising	Very negative but rising 7-☐
3-☐ High and rising	Little negative and rising 8-☐
4-☐ Very high and rather stable	Little negative and stable 9-☐
5-☐ Deteriorating	Deteriorating 10-☐

GEDANKEN EXPERIMENTS

A *gedanken* experiment is a thought experiment—what physicists do when they cannot perform the real experiment. Suppose we went to Microsoft and circulated the above question among employees and stockholders. It is safe to assume that in the late 1990s they were all optimistic rather than pessimistic concerning Microsoft's future. This already positions Microsoft on the early half of its overall curve. But, compared with a few years earlier, is the average optimism increasing, decreasing, or stable at a high level? The answer to this question is less obvious. My guess is that the average optimism at Microsoft is relatively lower today than it was in 1992 to 1993. If this is true, Microsoft finds itself in an early summer season—position 5 in Fig. 2.5—a few years before its zenith, the period with the highest growth rate. If, however, optimism in the Microsoft ranks has been steadily rising, the company is in position 3, early spring, not yet one-fifth its final size.

Now let us apply this approach to the U.S. economy. Inflation was rock-bottom low for at least 3 years beginning with 1993. This makes the value of money stable at a high level, position 4, with late 1997 corresponding to late spring. The implication is that the economic cycle is about one-third completed and has a season of *at least* 7 years. Assuming it is *equal* to 7 years, here are some insights that could guide financial decisions:

- The highest rate of economic growth should be expected around 1999, to be followed by the beginning of another recession.
- Inflation will begin rising again but will hit a record high only after 2002.
- The beginning of this economic growth cycle (its first winter) was around 1987.
- According to the recommendations in Chap. 2, the smart American investor in 1997 should be generally buying shares and—to a lesser extent—commodities and selling bonds.

The S-shaped curve is a visualization of the natural law that governs growth in competition. This curve depicts the size—the population—attained by a certain time: *how far you have gone.* The second visualization of the same law is the bell-shaped curve representing the rate of growth, the life cycle. This curve is linked to how much momentum you have acquired: *how difficult it will be to stop you.* The third visualization is the up-and-down-and-up curve. It is linked to the force that drives the growth process: *the promise for the future.*

The predictive power associated with these curves comes from their symmetry. Popular wisdom incorporated in such proverbs as "Easy come, easy go" and "Early ripe, early rot," reflects the fact that, on the surface, a life cycle is symmetric. Many companies that rose rapidly declined equally rapidly. An example is the People's Express experiment in air travel, which went up and down in a few years. Another example, of longer time scale, is DEC, which impressed the information technology industry equally with its rise as with its decline. IBM's life cycle is also symmetric, but it is very slow moving; it may take 150 years to go from beginning to end.

When quantitatively exploited, the natural growth law allows us to "see around corners." I successfully predicted the curbing of the increase in the number of deaths from AIDS in the United States from data up to 1988, a time when the disease depicted a galloping exponential growth, and alarmists were predicting the end of the human species.[7]

The predictive power associated with the questionnaire on future prospects comes from the fact that deep down inside we know important things in an emotional way. Our knowledge may lack mathematical precision, but it unquestionably distinguishes optimism from pessimism, euphoria from anxiety, relaxation from stress. It also tells us whether the change is for the better or for the worse.

LEONARDO DA VINCI WAS AHEAD OF THE ARISTOCRATS

The qualities attributed above to the different stages of growth are chosen as archetypes. The essential message is that the top priority changes with time. Excellence, quality, and leadership will naturally be cherished at all times. Yet it is appropriate to cherish them more in the summer season. The first year a car manufacturer brings out a new engine— or a computer manufacturer a new technology—customers do not get top performance. Improvements follow and peak during the model's summer. Similarly, innovation, creativity, and entrepreneurship are of objective value. Yet they are more appropriate in winter than in any other season. These characterizations should be understood in *relative* terms. Research organizations (for example, Bell Labs) are rich in innovation and creativity. Certification and control agencies (for example, the Food and Drug Administration) display a more bureaucratic character. But in one way or another, they all go through seasons, during which their characteristics will be *relatively* accentuated or suppressed with the passage of time.

Lawrence M. Miller in his book *Barbarians to Bureaucrats* assigned management roles to the various life-cycle stages of an enterprise. He put the prophet in the very beginning of the growth process—the early winter—and progressed through the crusader, the builder, the administrator, the bureaucrat, and finally the aristocrat as the enterprise enters decline—fall. These colorful images have the same flavor as the seasons metaphor. Miller missed, however, the Leonardo da Vincis, the people who bridge the gap between aristocrats and prophets.

Also related to the seasons metaphor is Slywotzky's concept of value migration. He argues that value migrates away from outmoded business designs to new ones that are better able to satisfy customers' priorities. He defines three phases of value migration[8]:

• In the *value inflow* phase, when a company starts to absorb value from other parts of the industry because the company's business design is superior to that of other companies. Microsoft and EDS are in this phase.

• During *stability,* value remains in the company's business design but no new value flows in. DuPont seems to be in such a phase.

- In the *value outflow* phase, when value starts to move away from a company's traditional activities toward business designs that more effectively meet evolving customer priorities. DEC and Bethlehem Steel find themselves in such a phase.

Slywotzky's three phases correspond to the seasons of spring, summer, and fall. Surprisingly, he makes no room for winter. Like Miller, he underestimates the critical evolutionary stage that follows the decline of the old and precedes the growth of the new. Slywotzky thus deprives CEOs of a focal point for a company turnaround, which, difficult as it may be, has a probability of happening naturally only during winter.

GROWTH FROM CHAOS AND CHAOS FROM GROWTH

- Fiascoes and failures should not be overlooked. They could herald future markets.

- In every supplier-receiver relationship, the season of each side must be considered.

- The right thing to do in *any* situation is mostly the opposite of what proved right two seasons ago.

For most of this century, scientists have not left economists at peace. Theory makers like to tear down and rebuild the work of their predecessors. Benoit Mandelbrot and more recent chaos scientists have argued that equilibrium and orderly growth are only the tip of the iceberg. The true richness of our world comes from the noisy, apparently random behavior encountered in the unpredictable patterns of currency movements and market reactions. In his best-selling *Chaos*, James Gleick explains that chaos fans are not interested in steady growth processes. They concentrate on the fluctuations that become prominent whenever the growth rate drops to zero. Through fractals* popularized via

---

*Fractals are irregular patterns that reveal an identical structure when zooming in and out. They are a consequence of a different geometry that has structure at multiple levels.

beautiful computer-generated pictures, chaos scientists have succeeded in extracting some order out of randomness. They want to believe that their theory contains all we need to know about markets. But practicing professionals remain skeptical.

Extreme swings of the pendulum typically straddle a wise intermediate position. The fact is that order and randomness coexist at all times, merely shifting their role as protagonist. During a high-growth period—summer season—the direction of growth is well defined, order dominates, and the fluctuations play a minimal role. But in a period of general stagnation—winter season—the fluctuations are all we see; in fact, they become very prominent, giving rise to a state of chaos. This state of chaos reflects the random trial-and-error search that people and organizations undertake to reestablish new growth paths.

Sustained growth is not a steady and uniform process. It consists of successive S-shaped steps, each of which represents a well-defined amount of growth. Every step is associated with a market niche that opened following a technological breakthrough, a major innovation, or some other fundamental change. Growth steps are punctuated by periods of chaos. Both theoretical and practical evidence exists for the chaotic fluctuations sketched freehand in Figs. 1-7, 2-1, and 2-2.

THE BEGINNING OF CHAOS

The relative order associated with the summer season of the growth process and the chaos associated with the winter season can be theoretically proved by using the fact that everything in nature is discrete.[1] When the analytical mathematical expression of the S-curve is cast into a discrete formulation, instabilities emerge at both ends of the growth process. In Fig. 3-1 we see the onset of chaos, for a certain combination of the parameter values. At this point, chaos is not yet fully installed, but there is an important oscillation in the beginning and at the end of the growth process. In real-life situations we cannot see the early oscillation completely, because negative values have no physical meaning. We see, however, a precursor followed by an accelerated growth rate, an overshoot of the ceiling, and finally erratic fluctuations. These features correspond to real phenomena. Accelerated growth is a catching-up effect, usually attributed to pent-up demand. The overshoot is a typical introduction into the steady state. As for the precursor, it is often considered a fiasco, unfairly so.

MAKING AN S-CURVE DISCRETE

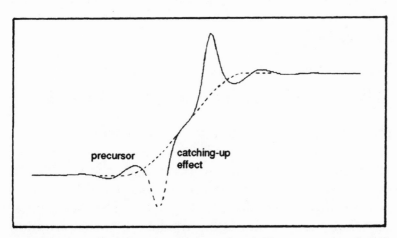

FIGURE 3-1. One of the first patterns obtained by putting an S-shaped curve in a discrete mathematical form. The deviations from the familiar S-curve demonstrate the early catching-up effect, the precursor, and the overshoot.

In 1993 DEC launched a personal computer model built with the company's powerful 64-bit Alpha microprocessor. Despite high expectations and the product's outstanding performance, sales disappointed even the pessimists. Two years later, the product was considered a failure. A variety of explanations were given—such as the lack of compatibility with software applications—and DEC went back to building personal computers with the traditional Intel chips. In the light of Fig. 3-1, DEC should have pursued the Alpha PC business line, treating the first unsuccessful model as a precursor rather than as a failure. The 64-bit technology had demonstrated that it survived infant mortality by becoming well established in larger computers. It was reasonable to expect that the technology would eventually downsize to personal computers, by which time demand would accelerate (the catching-up effect) and favor the manufacturers that were ready with the product.

Fiascoes and failures should not always be taken at face value. They can herald new markets, particularly if other well-established growth processes corroborate such an interpretation.

A LARGE-SCALE HISTORICAL EXAMPLE

A commonsense explanation associates business summer seasons with conservatism and tight control, in the spirit of not changing something that works well. At the same time, during the winter season, an erratic trial-and-error search for new growth opportunities gives rise to chaotic fluctuations. A naive but illuminating model for the alternation between order and chaos is the image of an elderly person who with shaking hands tries to draw an S-shaped curve. During the flat early part of the curve his trembling hand produces visible jagged peaks and troughs, but during the sharp upward move the fluctuations from the trembling become masked by the well-pronounced trend.

But the most pragmatic justification for expecting order to lead into chaos and back comes from historical observation. An example in a large time frame is the world economy, as evidenced by the evolution of energy consumption. Per-capita energy consumption worldwide is seven times greater today than it was 150 years ago. This increase took place, not at a steady, uniform rate or even in a random fashion, but in two well-defined steps. The first step ended around 1920 with a period of stagnation that lasted about two decades. The second energy consumption step was completed around 1975, and we have not yet witnessed the beginning of a third step. There can be little doubt, however, that this indicator will soon enjoy a new growth phase, considering the insatiable appetite for energy in the West and the dire need for industrial growth in the developing world.

Energy consumption correlates in an unambiguous way with industrial development and economic prosperity. The profile of the energy curve over time eloquently points out two chaotic low-growth periods, one centered around the mid-1930s and another one around 1990. These economic depressions echo Kondratieff's economic cycle.

Many economists today dispute the existence of long economic waves, perhaps because most proponents of long waves have relied on monetary and econometric indicators—labels that, like price tags, are unreliable for assigning lasting value. Inflation and currency fluctuations owing to politicoeconomic circumstances can have a large, unpredictable effect on monetary indicators. Extreme swings have been observed. For example, Van Gogh died poor, although his paintings are worth a fortune today. The number of artworks he produced has not changed since his death, nor has the amount of paint and canvas he used, or the total hours he put in. Counted in dollars, however, Van Gogh's work has increased tremendously.

Figure 3-2 provides evidence for a long cycle on the basis of physical indicators alone, such as energy consumption expressed in tons of coal-equivalent.[2] I have studied and documented in my book *Predictions* many cyclical phenomena resonating with the energy consumption cycle. For each human endeavor considered—production, consumption, manufacturing, construction, creativity, productivity,

NATURAL GROWTH ALTERNATING WITH STATES OF CHAOS

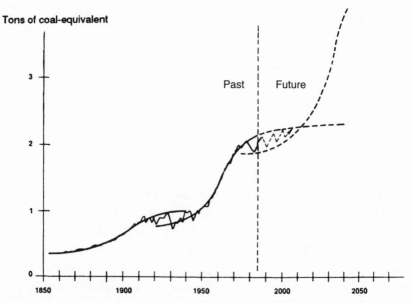

FIGURE 3-2. The per-capita annual energy consumption worldwide: data, fits, and a scenario for the future.

criminality, and the like—I used data expressed in their proper units, not by their prices. Through all these observations I was able to determine this cycle's period to be equal to 56 years, give or take 2 years.

Several theoretical explanations have been offered for the origin of a long economic wave. In the 1930s, Joseph A. Schumpeter at Harvard put forth socioeconomic theories, such as the rapid growth of leading sectors and the clustering of technological innovations. More recently, Jay Forrester at MIT was able to reproduce the same long wave with his sophisticated system dynamics model, which studied major shifts in private sector incentives for investing in capital plant, borrowing, and saving. Finally, in *Predictions*, I offer two more hypotheses for the existence of such a long wave. One has to do with periodic changes of the climate, the other relates to the mean life span of a person's commercially active career.[3]

But let us go back to the energy consumption picture with its two low-growth periods around the 1930s and the 1990s. During these winter seasons the chaotic state is manifested through bottom-up, bursting cultural forces that lead to segmentation, decentralization, and horizontal markets. Leadership becomes ineffective. In contrast, during the high-growth period, top-down vision-driven forces tend to unify and integrate, vertically or otherwise. Predictably, the two chaotic states are associated with periods of low economic growth but also periods of discovery and innovation. Difficult times make people inventive. A host of important innovations in the 1930s set the pace for a recovery that led to the high-growth period of the 1950s and the 1960s. To mention a few such innovations: television (1936), Kodachrome (1935), synthetic rubber (1932), wrinkle-free fabrics (1932), helicopters (1936), rockets (1935), automatic transmissions (1939), power steering (1930), magnetic tape recording (1937), diesel locomotives (1934), ballpoint pens (1938), radar (1934), plexiglass (1935), fluorescent lighting (1934), and nylon perlon (1938).[4] By analogy, the 1990s can expect a multitude of industry-generating innovations that trigger a recovery and another economic summer early next century. Examples of well-positioned candidates are fax machines, portable computers, cellular telephones, optical fibers, optical disks, tomography, high-bandwidth communication networks, all-invading intelligent microprocessors, space shuttle, biosciences, gene technology, robotics, and high-temperature superconductivity.

The depressed world economy of the 1990s was responsible for the widespread breaking up large enterprises into smaller ones. During the early 1990s, DuPont reorganized itself by creating 22 autonomous strategic business units. IBM did something similar in the United Kingdom with 13 autonomous business units and, further, created entirely new companies for the PC division and some of its services. In contrast, industries that despite the world economic climate found themselves in a high-growth season—for example, the telecom industry—prospered from corporate alliances, mergers, acquisitions, and other unifying mechanisms.

Because different business seasons dictate distinctly different behavior, successful strategic actions become telltale signals for the season a company is in. When we read that chemical empires in continental Europe, such as Bayer and Hoechst of Germany and Rhone-Poulenc of France, spun off fibers, bulk and specialty chemicals, pharmaceuticals, and agriculture into legally independent subsidiaries, we could have concluded that the European chemical industry was in difficulty, even if we were not knowledgeable about the industry. By contrast, the announcement of impressive long-range plans by MCI Communications Corporation insinuated a healthy balance sheet. Long-range strategies are characteristic of a summer business season.

IN POLITICS AS IN BUSINESS

The association of segmentation with low growth and unification with high growth is a general phenomenon that extends beyond the world of business. An example is the politicization process in Europe. When communism collapsed in the mid-1990s, the Eastern European countries found themselves drifting into a state of chaos. Appropriately, they were torn apart by bottom-up forces, decentralizing, segmenting, subdividing, searching for identity and political system, and, in general, exploring all directions including extreme ones, such as private police units in Moscow and murderous belligerencies in former Yugoslavia. Bottom-up forces make leadership unstable. Exceptional leaders like Mikhail Gorbachev, Eduard Shevardnadze, and Boris Yeltsin proved rather ineffective in controlling the strong and turbulent cultural forces. Oleg Bogomolov, Yeltsin's economic adviser, candidly remarked in 1993: "I find out where politics are in Russia through graffiti on the walls. One day I see on a wall, 'Give us back socialism.' The next day there is an addition, 'Socialism never existed.' The third day a new addition, 'Give us back what never existed.'"

In contrast, Western European countries have undergone considerable political development and enjoy a certain maturity as a result. Mediocre leaders have no difficulty surviving there. The name of the political game is unity, as in the European Union (E.U.). Such centralizing actions are timely and portend a dominant role in the world economy during the next economic development phase. (This promise becomes enhanced by the formidable need for development of E.U.'s next-door neighbors, the Central and Eastern European countries.)

THE COLLAPSE OF THE
COMMUNIST EMPIRE

The ultimate undoing of a forecaster is to predict something after it has happened. Well, my work revolves around innovative forecasting techniques, and here I am about to present arguments demonstrating that the collapse of communism could have been predicted with devilish precision as early as the 1960s. What makes me indulge in such an unprofessional exercise is the fact that recently one more person threw at me the by now classic remark: "Who could have ever predicted the fall of the Berlin wall?" His comment was the last straw.

As mentioned earlier, the chaotic period begins with the end of the growth process. At the same time, life cycles are generally symmetric. Communist rule began in 1917. It peaked 40 years later, in the mid-1950s, when the Soviet Union successfully competed with and often surpassed the United States (for example, with Sputnik in 1957). A symmetric life cycle would position the end of communism another 40 years later, in the mid-1990s. The headline-making event, the collapse of the Berlin wall in 1989, took place in a sharp discontinuous way, reflecting the first large fluctuation of the chaotic state that sets in as the natural growth process approaches completion. With the end of the process anticipated in the mid-1990s, chaotic tremors are to be expected several years earlier. These are rather accurate predictions for the collapse of communism and the Berlin wall. They ensue from a rigorous and precise reckoning. They could have been made as early as the 1960s, when it became clear that the Soviet Union was already over its peak. The Soviets had begun losing, first in 1963 with the Cuban missile crisis, then in 1969 with the moon race that was doomed for lack of funds. The Soviets could not afford adequate testing of their superior rocket, and it exploded during the critical launch.

The fall of the Berlin wall punctuated the end of the Communist growth curve and signaled the beginning of the chaotic phase. It will take a while for free market forces to become established there, however. According to the seasons metaphor, the four seasons have equal duration—in this case, 20 years (one-fourth of the 80-year life cycle of the Soviet bloc). In that light, the present winter in Russia could easily last until 2010.

THE RISE AND FALL OF A COMPUTER GIANT

During its 35-year history, DEC evolved through many successive growth steps. The four most recent steps can be seen in Fig. 3-3, which shows the evolution of the company's employee population during the last 20 years. The trend in employee numbers closely correlates to the company's performance and is a better indicator of profitability than is net operating revenue.

The first three steps are rather similar and are characterized by positive growth. Each step spans about 4 years and undergoes periods of high and low growth. The fourth step is characterized by negative growth—that is, a downward-pointing S-curve. But here again the rate of decline undergoes rapid and slow periods.

Negative growth and positive growth go through similar phases—seasons—and a few basic seasonal attributes remain unchanged between the two. For example, both positive and negative summers are characterized by centralization, leadership, top-down management with increased central control, and bureaucratic procedures. Other attributes—such as

THE EVOLUTION OF THE NUMBER OF EMPLOYEES AT DEC

FIGURE 3-3. The evolution of DEC's workforce during the last 20 years. Three similar well-defined rising steps show alternating periods of high (summer) and low (winter) growth. The hand-drawn fluctuations superimposed to the low-growth periods indicate the chaotic nature of winters. The thick line is an S-curve fit to the declining phase. The data come from annual company reports. See the text for a chronology of events associated with the seasons.

those concerning pricing, profits, and long-range planning—become reversed. For springs and falls, too, some attributes remain unchanged and others reverse. During positive spring there is learning and a need for specialists to design and build, but during a negative spring specialists are needed to restructure and reduce. At the same time, positive spring is characterized by investments, whereas negative spring is characterized by disinvestments.

Companies reorganize frequently. They swing from centralization to decentralization and from integration to segmentation, a pattern that may seem contradictory but exists because the company grows in steps. DEC's management followed this pattern as the company went through the growth steps shown in Fig. 3-3. (The study was carried out in the beginning of 1994 and makes use of no private information.)

1979–1980, summer of first step: vertical integration, centralization. Software becomes a business activity. Product lines and functions (stovepipes) become popular. Services are integrated at the corporate level. Hardware architectures become consolidated into one, the VAX.

1981–1982, winter between steps 1 and 2: horizontal organization, decentralization. Product lines drop out of favor. Engineering and technical support are spread over several geographies across Europe. There are discussions about making Europe autonomous.

1983–1984, summer of second step: advertising, market expansion, vertical organization, leadership, integration. Heavy advertising and market expansion efforts are evident, and the first DECVille, the largest show up to that time of a hardware manufacturer, is implemented. Functions become important once again. Europe is unified into one entity. With its own CEO, Pierre Carlo Falotti, DEC Europe produces its own long-range plan. Software services become integrated with hardware maintenance.

1985, winter between steps 2 and 3: entrepreneurship, decentralization. Entrepreneurial initiatives, such as business consulting, become income-producing rather than advisory. Order-history databases and systems development are decentralized across Europe.

1987, summer of third step: long-range strategic planning, integration, centralization. A proliferation of centralized think-tank activities around long-term strategies emerges. The importance of network/communications is recognized; telecommunications becomes a worldwide strategic business, reinforcing the tradition of product lines.

1989–1991, winter between steps 3 and 4: entrepreneurship, segmentation, horizontal organization.

Entrepreneurial business models and empowerment of front-line managers are new themes. Strategic business units (SBUs) are created. Cross-functional operations (horizontal organizations) become popular. Digital Enterprise Europe (DEE) is created in Europe as a daughter company to target small and medium-size enterprises.

1992–1993, "negative summer" of step 4: centralization, leadership. Chief executive officer and founder, Ken Olsen, is replaced by Bob Palmer. Most functions become centralized at corporate level. SBUs fall out of favor.

1995–1996, "negative winter" between steps 4 and 5. A *relative* return to decentralization, entrepreneurship, and empowerment is likely.

There is general coherence between DEC's management actions and behaviors according to the seasons metaphor. Even during times of negative growth, the trends of management decisions at DEC swung from decentralization to centralization, from innovation and entrepreneurship to control and conservatism as the rate of decline passed from low to high. During the "negative summer" of 1992–1993, bureaucracies came into existence only for the purpose of expediently accommodating the population-reduction process.

As this declining step came to a conclusion, a slowdown in the reduction of employee numbers was expected during 1995 and 1996. The fact that a winter season was coming up meant that once again DEC's management was likely to turn, in *relative* terms, toward its front-line managers, empowering and encouraging them to take initiatives. Time has proven the above projections correct. DEC's employee population was stable during 1996–1997 and there has been a noticeable relaxation of tight centralized control. Entrepreneurial activities by local management are becoming progressively more visible. More declining steps in the number of employees cannot be excluded in the future, even if the company wanders into profitability. As a matter of fact, more declining steps would be expected from Fig. 3-3, if we zoom back and look at the overall graph as a single large-scale life cycle.

The company's critical period was the winter of 1989 to 1991. At that time, an upward growth step would have been possible, and indeed had happened many times before. But that winter was more significant; it coincided with a world-wide economic winter. The situation called for more dramatic entrepreneurship and change. DEC had to go further toward becoming a different species—for example, by focusing on services, which at the time were in a spring season. Instead, the company retreated into hardware, and was dragged into a downturn.

REVOLUTIONS AND RE-EVOLUTIONS

In natural growth processes, chaos gives way to order just as spring follows winter and leads into summer. In nature these things happen by themselves, but in the marketplace people tend to interfere—constructively sometimes, less so at other times. Launching new products is not a complicated process. The difficult transition period between successive products presents no real problem when the overall ability to innovate (technology) is not yet exhausted. In any case, portfolios of several products, at different seasons each, ensure continuous growth for the company. But if we look at the whole company as one product, its rebirth is more difficult to achieve.

Turning a company around is an almost impossible task, because it involves diverting a process from a declining natural course. In nature, such diversions do not happen. No species, unaided, ever succeeded in halting its own extinction. Yet most companies embark on this attempt. They reorganize, replacing much of their personnel up through the management team. But in the end, only a few companies succeed. Product substitution proceeds successfully only for truly differentiated products. Similarly, a company turnaround succeeds only if the changes are so profound that the transformation is tantamount to creating a different company. That is why the chief executive—sometimes the founder—usually has to go. The old culture has to die in order for a new one to grow. The board's primary concern should be to make sure that the planned changes do not fall short of transforming the organization into a new "species."

In this light, a merger like the one of Burroughs and Sperry into Unisys back in 1986 was doomed from the beginning, for two reasons. First, at the time both companies were experiencing difficulties—a season of fall—so that to unite was not the recommended evolutionary course. Second, there was no radical reshuffling of personnel or culture to ensure a transformation of the species. The consequences could have been predicted. When graphed historically, the phasing-out trajectory of the combined market share follows a smooth S-shaped decline with no deviations around 1986.

The S-shaped pattern of a natural growth process indicates the way organisms and populations grow and decline in nature. It represents nature's ways of wisdom, or ways of least resistance—the most economic paths. It is unwise to attempt to go against them. Policies cannot be made across the board according to the company's overall performance. Individual attention must be paid to the evolutionary phase of each department, function, service, or even product, because they are not generally in sync.

During the 1980s and the 1990s, major computer manufacturers (such as IBM and DEC) expanded their operations to include consulting services. These new activities, with their own growth characteristics, found themselves in a season different from that of hardware sales. Consequently, the management initiatives for these divisions had to be quite different, and in some cases awkwardly so. With products in fall and services in spring, some things are easier than others. For example, it is relatively straightforward to disinvest from products to invest in services. But it is less obvious to evolve toward entrepreneurship and segmentation for the former, and at the same time move toward integration and centralization for the latter. The difficulty may be the most important argument for a clean-cut cessation of service activities, shifting them into a separate company (for example, the creation of Andersen Consulting by Arthur Andersen).

IF SUMMER IS HERE, CAN FALL BE FAR BEHIND?

In some cultures if you ask a store owner how business is going, you are likely to get the following response: "Tomorrow it will be worse." In his book *The Age of Paradox*, Charles Handy warns managers to be vigilant for the turning point, the time when summer comes to an end and a declining growth rate tends to be overlooked. But it is inefficient to gear continuously for disaster. It is possible to anticipate the turning point with sufficient accuracy and prepare for its consequences *in time*.[5] What is more difficult—and can become a cardinal mistake—is not to recognize and accept the downtrend.

In late 1987 I was advising the CEO of DEC International about the prospects of future growth for the

European market, the company's fastest-growing region. I was relatively new in the company, and my methods were considered revolutionary. DEC had been accustomed to annual growth rates of 30 to 40 percent. My forecast for 1988 was a mere 15 percent. My own advisers—senior to me in age and years with the company—argued vehemently against this result and put pressure on me to present a figure closer to twice that to the CEO. Finally, after using all the margin that uncertainties would permit, I presented a 1988 forecast of 20 percent. The CEO was displeased and dismissed it. But a month later, during the end-of-year address, the CEO talked to the employees following a trip to the United States. There, over the crowd and in between applause, he discreetly turned toward me and said, "I am afraid you are right." In fact, DEC's summer was over.

But winters do not necessarily last forever. Winter is an opportunity to search for and set new directions, and a chance for decision makers to exercise their free will. During summers they cannot do that because they are obliged to optimize around the established successful course. If managers accurately determine what business season they have entered, how long it will last, and their position in it, they can then use the seasons metaphor as a guide for setting strategies that favor the rise of another spring.

Management needs to become aware of the season of each and every major unit of the enterprise. The various units must interrelate harmoniously, but they may find themselves in different seasons and thus in need of different management styles. Like a marketer caring for a portfolio of products, top management must nurse its business units individually. At times, this may seem like an impossible task. Some units may need to be organized horizontally, others in stovepipes; some may be in need of innovation and redesign, others may call for tighter control and total quality management. The most dangerous situation may arise when a newly appointed chief executive, convinced of the merits of empowerment, entrepreneurship, core competencies, and business process reengineering, faces a business unit that finds itself in the early growth phases of a promising market. If the CEO is not capable of instantly switching mentalities, it might be in the unit's best interest to be spun off as an independent entity.

WHERE ON THE CURVE ARE YOUR CLIENTS?

You probably have a fairly good general idea of the overall season your company is presently in. The season's duration is less obvious. The situation with your different departments may be even less obvious. But still less known are the seasons of your customers, and more important, of those out there who are not yet your customers.

In every relationship, the disposition of the two partners is of prime importance. In a customer-supplier relationship, an understanding of the seasons can point out opportunities and reveal pitfalls. When both vendor and client are doing well—a summer-summer situation—profitability is at a record high, but only for established relationships. It is extremely difficult to win over new customers, because satisfied people are not looking for change. In contrast, a winter-winter position is certainly not a profitable period, but it is a time that offers unique opportunities for striking up new friendships.

Intermediate positions are more intricate to evaluate, particularly when both client and supplier belong to the same company. DEC, for example, had traditionally offered hardware products as well as the maintenance services these products required. Over the decades, the service business grew relative to the product sales, moving from 15 percent of all revenue in 1975 to 50 percent by 1994. Services were in a late-spring, early-summer season, in contrast to hardware, which in 1994 was in a late-fall, early-winter season. Such a situation calls for dissociating the hardware from the maintenance business. Indeed the company did so by progressively expanding its service offerings to cover maintenance on machines from other vendors. But the decision was slow and poorly implemented, and, moreover, some of the new business was outsourced. If adequate attention had been paid to the seasonal evolution of DEC's service business, management could have anticipated and planned for growth. Furthermore, the new business would have been optimized via the appropriate policies—for example, centralization, investments, and vertical integration, policies that were falling into disfavor at that time in an environment dominated by a mentality appropriate for hardware. Optimizing the hardware independently from the service business could have yielded unexpected—yet profitable—combinations. It may have turned out to be more profitable, for example, to outsource the maintenance on some of DEC's own products, while letting the profit-reaping service organization realize its growth potential largely on the machines of other manufacturers.

Maps such as those in Fig. 3-4 provide guidelines for setting relationship strategies. To target customers, you need to accurately position clients and vendors and then study closely the three-dimensional surfaces. A quick—and obvious—rule of thumb is: If you want to go for profitability, concentrate on old customers—in particular, those that are doing best (the fast-growing segment of the familiar mar-

THE PROFITABILITY WITH OLD CUSTOMERS

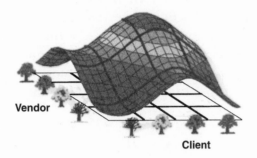

Vendor

Client

THE PROFITABILITY OF WINNING NEW CUSTOMERS

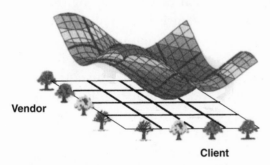

Vendor

Client

FIGURE 3-4.   Profitability is highest when both client and vendor are in a summer season (top). The probability of establishing new commercial relationships is highest when both client and vendor are in a winter season (bottom).

ket). If you want to increase your customer base, target the firms that are experiencing a winter (next-wave firms). The economic climate and the relative size and abundance of your customers will help you set your priorities.

But such maps can also be used internally, even with elements operating in different time frames. For example, technology feeds the launching of new products, but the life cycle of technology is much longer than the life cycle of products. A two-dimensional surface like that of Fig. 3-4, with technology on one axis and products on the other, will look like curved corrugated cardboard. It will point out the times—a product's fall coinciding with the technology's winter—when product replacement will be most problematic.

SUCCESS IN ALL SEASONS

Many of the actions that are right for the season are commonsense and intuitive and generally correspond to familiar management policies. The critical factor is timing. Failures result from good decisions that are ill-timed. As seasons change, even persisting trends go through phases of acceleration and deceleration. Competition, for example, has long been tightening its noose worldwide as a consequence of increasing populations and standards of living. But competition should ease *relatively* during the period of rising worldwide economic growth at the turn of the century.

By varying the time frame, we can see a more complete picture. The elements of an enterprise—products, departments, business units, and customers—generally cease to exist at the end of their life cycle. Associating seasons with the passage of time sets the scene for "immortality" and allows us to see things from a higher level. We can then identify those elements and substitution processes that, with timely support, are likely to revive the enterprise.

The cyclical variation from winter to summer, from high growth to low growth, from a niche that becomes exhausted to a niche that just opens up, becomes the engine of evolution and offers life-giving capabilities. Potential differences act as sources of energy, and the wider the swing between the extremes, the richer the field to be exploited. Diversity in culture, geography, skills, and state of development is a strength to be sought after. The wise person will seek out and feed on potential differences. For example, Western society is reaching a level of saturation in economic development, an autumn season. At the same time, Southeast Asia and the Far East (Singapore, Shanghai) are experiencing economic expansion, a spring season. That is why so many Western firms and individuals have been shifting their energy and attention from West to East, leaving behind a curve that is flattening for a curve that is becoming progressively steep. They are like entrepreneurial scientists who give up a classical discipline that is approaching saturation (such as physics or chemistry) for a cross-disciplinary endeavor that finds itself in infancy with much growth potential ahead (such as biochemistry or management science).

The successes of yesterday become the problems of today. This is so because learning, creativity, and productivity are natural growth processes associated with the filling or the emptying of a niche. Consequently, following much success, the respective niche becomes either exhausted or completed. In either case no more exploitation activities are possible, and the rate of growth drops to zero. At the same time, this winter stagnation triggers entrepreneurial activities that will define and promote new directions of growth. The problems of today give rise to the opportunities of tomorrow. In each season, the typical behavior observed is also the correct one. Paths of least resistance ensure efficient survival. If what is done is not conducive to survival, the organism ceases to exist and the behavior is no longer observable.

What normally gets done is what *should* be done. Nature has a good record of doing things in the best possible way. Here are some examples. Light rays bend at certain angle when they enter water, reaching the object they illuminate *in the shortest possible time*. A tossed stone follows a parabolic trajectory that *minimizes the amount of action* involved. Surface tension gives a soap bubble the shape of a perfect sphere, enclosing a certain volume in the *smallest possible* surface. Machiavelli was right. To act in accordance with the spirit of the season is to follow a path of least resistance—consequently, to do something in the best possible way. This is not a fatalistic or pessimistic statement. Growth and prosperity do follow the most economic path.

THE PHILOSOPHER'S STONE

The seasons metaphor can be encapsulated into an operational definition for a philosopher's stone. In the alchemists' tradition, the philosophers' stone was a desired object that would tell you the right thing to do, whatever the situation.* The version offered here calls for taking three steps before you respond to change in your business (at the level of a product, service, unit, department, function, or company):

1. To the best of your ability make a guess about what season you are in, where in the season you are, and how long it will last. (There are sophisticated tools to help you.[6] However, the questionnaire in Where Are You on the Curve? in Chap. 2 is a good start.)
2. Go back two seasons and identify activities that proved successful then.

---

*It is a hasty simplification to say that alchemists' main goal was to find a way to turn cheap metals into gold. The alchemical work was symbolic and esoteric, aiming at ultimate knowledge and eventual "awakening." The philosopher's stone was a key substance in achieving that goal.

3. Opt for the opposite of those activities. Check your decisions and enhance them with the detailed attributes of the seasons listed in Chap. 2.

EXAMPLES

Here are some generic applications of the philosopher's stone. You will need to develop them in depth and adapt them to your particular situation.

JOBS.   If you lose your job (that is, find yourself in a professional winter), consider becoming entrepreneurial and opportunistic. Take risks, break rules, and explore all directions. These behaviors are opposite to those that helped you succeed when your job was at its zenith. You were then conservative, conformist, obedient, and unidirectional. You worked long days, asking no questions: you work less but question more now.

PRODUCTS.   During the early stages of a product's life cycle—winter—the salesforce is opportunistic. Two seasons later—summer—the opposite behavior is appropriate. Sales operations invariably become centralized and regulated, making use of automated procedures for price quotation and order intake.

ENTERPRISES.   Many computer firms, such as IBM and DEC, segmented and reorganized themselves horizontally when the computer industry entered a low-growth period—winter—in the early 1990s. This was a behavior opposite to the vertical integration and stovepipe structures they had adopted two seasons earlier, during the industry's summer in the early 1980s.

LIFE.   People in the fall season of their lives wonder about what to do next. They should consider the opposite of what really helped them during their spring season. Youngsters typically benefit from learning activities such as reading, schooling, and apprenticeships. Older people then, even if they have the opportunity to go back to school, will benefit more from writing, teaching, and coaching. But it must all be tailored to the particular situation. For example, a young student who is poor should benefit from a scholarship; an older person who is rich will benefit from contributing to a scholarship fund.

THE BIG PICTURE

- "Competition is the creator and the regulator."
  Heraclitus, 500 B.C.
- Coevolution—adapting to meet each other's needs—works miracles. It will become more important in the future.
- Forecasting techniques too are seasonal.

If by some supernatural circumstances you could have a single wish, what wish would you make? Would you ask for gold, health, beauty? More evolved thinking suggests asking for the ability to fulfill wishes. In other words, position yourself on a higher level that gives you access to a new dimension. A dictum such as "Things will always change" implies that at some point things will find themselves in a state of stability. Otherwise there is something that does not change: the state of permanent change! If this statement sounds a bit circular, consider that scientific research has also ventured in this direction. Avant-garde biologists today are talking about the evolution of the evolution.

THE EVOLUTION OF THE EVOLUTION

Darwinian natural selection seems to involve discontinuities, stages in which cooperation replaces competition, yielding a sizable step forward in evolution. Much like the image of cascading S-curves in which states of chaos alternate with states of order, evolution goes through stages of competition alternating with stages of cooperation.

Let us condense Darwin's theory into three words:

mutation—selection—diffusion[1]

Mutation is a random trial-and-error search usually encountered during chaotic periods when growth is low. *Selection* is the competitive process that singles out the best-fit mutations. *Diffusion* is the multiplication and spreading of these mutations into the available niche space, along S-shaped growth curves. Although the key word is *competition,* the power of the method relies upon large numbers. The larger the number of mutations, the higher the chance for success—that is, the chance for accidentally hitting upon "gifted" configurations. According to the Bible, when God wanted to ensure survival of the chosen people, he promised them that they would become more numerous than the grains of sand on the sea shore (Genesis).*

At the end of the diffusion process, as a niche becomes filled, low growth rates stimulate new mutations, and the process starts over again. Traditional Darwinian evolution then proceeds in incremental steps, cascading S-curves. Each step is associated with a mutation chosen because it demonstrated superiority over the alternatives.

But during the last 30 years, Darwinism has come under strong attack. Outspoken biologist Lynn Margulis says that "natural selection is the editor, not the author." It is a death mechanism that decides who will die and who will live. But such things as wings and eyes could never have evolved

---

*Cesare Marchetti points out that this number is much greater than 1000 billion. He then calculates that it is possible to reach this limit—200 times today's world population—without exhausting any basic resource, including the environment![2]

incrementally, because no intermediate state of development would have offered any advantages. Unless all the fine-tuning necessary for functionality is in place, eyes and wings are likely to be of little use. This argument has already been disputed. Nevertheless, Darwin himself agonized over how his theory would embrace the appearance of the eyeball. "The eye to this day gives me a cold shudder," he wrote to his American friend Asa Gray.[3] Kevin Kelly, executive editor of *Wired* magazine, documented many of the arguments and theories of the new biology in his book *Out of Control*. Margulis and the post-Darwinians, as Kelly calls them, argue that natural selection simply eliminates the ineffective. Death makes room for the new, but to say that death *causes* wings to be formed and eyeballs to work is incorrect.

Other mechanisms—such as symbiosis, mutual relationships, and coevolution—are responsible for rapid, creative, and sizable evolutionary steps. Cooperation unleashes a new dimension in evolution. A small amount of symbiotic coordination at the right time replaces an eon of minor alterations. In one mutual relationship, evolution could jump past a million years of individual trial and error. For example, membraned cells did not have to reinvent by trial and error over a billion years the clever process of photosynthesis and respiration worked out by some bacteria. Instead, they incorporated the bacteria as wholly owned subsidiaries working for the cells. They kidnapped the innovations.[4]

The increasing popularity of cross-disciplinary studies is a result of the same kind of mutual relationship. A new activity like management science incorporates at once knowledge accumulated over centuries by natural sciences such as biology, ecology, and physics. Despite decades of experience in jet aircraft design, the architects of the supersonic Concorde went back to study bird flight at the inception of their project. They shortened the time it would have taken for airplanes to evolve there via natural selection mechanisms. There is a large evolutionary step associated with the emergence of organisms or products enhanced by mutual or symbiotic relationships.

In a sense, when an evolutionary step involves the kidnapping of innovation, evolution is guided by a higher-level being. Natural selection among bacteria favors not the survival of the bacteria alone but also the survival of the host organism. If a parasite succeeds too well, the host dies, taking down with it the parasite itself. The weapons industry has for millennia evolved toward more effective elimination of the enemy—that is, survival of the species (in this case the different nations). When survival of the nation became assured with nuclear weapons, disarmament was adopted as a coevolutionary step guided by humanity as whole rather than individual nations. This reasoning resonates with James Lovelock's concept of Gaia. He argues that the exterior envelope of the earth should be considered as a living being, capable of self-regulation, and that the ensemble is more than the sum of the parts.[5] These are not poetic images. Coevolution is supported by the theory of complexity.

A steeply rising coevolutionary step is followed by a period during which evolution proceeds slowly, more traditionally, via the trial-and-error process of natural selection. Symbiosis and cooperation create order. Mutations and competition thrive on chaos. And this cycle repeats itself, making evolution evolve.

Evolution is not invariant over time. Kelly lists the various stages of evolution that the earth has gone through since its inception. At the very beginning, evolution favored the survival of anything stable. Stability permitted evolution to operate longer and generated further stability. At the next stage, evolution evolved *self-replicating* stabilities. Self-reproduction provided the possibility of error and variation. Evolution then evolved natural selection and unleashed its remarkable search power. Next, evolution gave rise to more complicated bodies and behaviors, bodies that reshaped themselves and animals that chose their own ecological niches. These choices led to a kind of bodily "learning." Learning hastened the next step: the evolution of a complex symbolic learning machine—the human brain—which itself evolved toward smarter forms. Today evolution favors those capable of learning.

God knows where evolution may evolve next. A likely course that evolution may take is self-direction. In *self-direction,* evolution itself chooses where it wants to evolve.[6] The British zoologist Richard Dawkins proposed a higher-level natural selection that favors a tendency to evolve in certain directions or even a tendency to evolve at all. In other words, evolution would choose not only to survive but also to further evolve.

The evolution of evolution is the power to change the rules of the game. When the change takes place, there is a jump. The rest of the time selection rules choose among random occurrences. The overall picture may well look like a long stream of cascading S-shaped steps: small ones associated with the mutation-based competitive traditional Darwinian evolution and large ones associated with the cooperative symbiotic innovation-kidnapping jumps. In a macroscopic time scale, this again is an alternation between states of relative order and chaos.

A strategy with limited look-ahead can be called *positive myopia.* Chess masters do not look far ahead to play excellent games. They work from rules of thumb that apply equally well to business, politics, technology, and life. Their advice is "Favor moves that increase options; shy away from moves that end well but require cutting off choices; work from strong positions that have many adjoining strong positions. Balance looking ahead to really paying attention to what is happening now on the whole board."[7]

The alternation between states of order and chaos makes positive myopia a winning strategy. Predictability is associated with one S-shaped step at a time. Prediction machinery need not see like a prophet to be of use. It need only detect limited patterns, such as S-shaped steps and periods of chaos. Once in an S-curve pattern, you know how things will evolve for a while. Linear projections constitute valid forecasting techniques, as long as you stay within a time window limited to the central segment of the S-step. During chaos, you follow your nose from one move to the next, and all you know is that before long, a step with well-defined direction will show up again. Valid forecasting techniques for this period are scenarios (for example, the celebrated multiple scenario playing of Shell) and other decision support techniques (for example, the competition-management methodology of Growth Dynamics) that help you identify the "chosen" direction before it becomes common knowledge. More on this in Chap. 6.

ZOOMING IN AND OUT

The danger associated with positive myopia is to miss far-reaching insights accessible via a bigger picture. The big picture is not just the cascading from one S-shaped step to the next. It is a cascade of cascades, an endless stream of S-curves alternating with periods of chaos, as described earlier. Would the corresponding life cycles—the rate of growth—be a regular oscillation? Does Kondratieff's cycle over the centuries tick like a clock, repeating its peaks and troughs at exact intervals? Are the random fluctuations of a few percent in magnitude observed during the last 200 years the only deviations possible? If that is the case, how do we explain the shortening of life cycles (of products, technologies, and so on), and the paradigm shift, progressively crowding humanity's significant transitions in recent history?[8]

A group of people linked by a common goal, interest, ability, or affiliation—for example, a company or an organization—will have its own S-shaped evolution. The individuals now play the role of the cells in a multicellular organism, and their assembly becomes the organism. The population in its entirety—that is, the organization itself—can be seen as an individual. The same is true for products. A group of products, each with its own life cycle, can be described by a similar but larger curve representing the *family* or the *technology* life cycle. If we zoom back further, we may find that many technologies come and go, succeeding each other the way products do. Thus we find a *fractal* aspect in the S-shaped natural growth pattern.[9] That is, zooming in or out, we obtain the same S-shaped pattern, and the only difference is the time frame (see Fig. 4-1).

S-curves are nested like Russian dolls. Consequently, there are many product seasons in one company season, many company seasons in one industry season, and many industry seasons in one global economy season. In all cases, the main characteristics of the social phenomena and human behaviors associated with a given season are similar. But there are nonobvious connections across the different levels of S-curves. For the sake of discussion, let us consider four levels of nested S-curves. Each level goes through natural growth steps with a life cycle of the same pattern but of different duration. A typical situation might be as follows:

THE FRACTAL NATURE OF NATURAL GROWTH

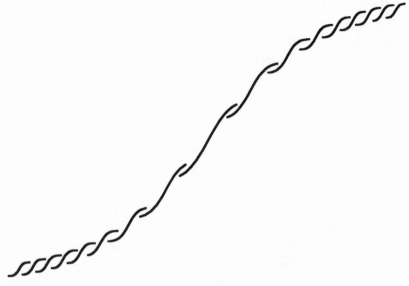

FIGURE 4-1. An overall S-shaped pattern decomposed into constituent S-shaped curves according to a rigorous procedure. The horizontal axis represents time.

Products consist of units sold and have a typical life cycle of 6 quarters.

Product families or *companies* consist of a set of related products and have a typical business cycle of 5 years—in the case of a product family, 5 years may be the duration of its life cycle.

Basic technologies or *industries* consist of a set of related product families or companies and have a typical cycle of 15 years.

The *economy* is the sum of all industries and has a cycle of 56 years.

S-curves at different levels are linked. For example, the high output of a summer season feeds the S-curves of one level below. That is why product replacement is least painful when the product family is in summer, just as the replacement of product families is least painful when the technology curve is in summer. Another link between S-curves of different levels occurs with innovation, which normally belongs in winter. Innovation in spring concerns the S-curves of one level below. For example, the spring of an industry brings product innovation. The spring of the economy brings industry innovation.

The graph in Fig. 4-1 has been constructed in a rigorous and quantitative way. The overall curve has a certain thickness within which the constituent S-curves must be contained. Redundant solutions are eliminated by requiring all constituent curves to belong to the same class. That is, they must all have the same slope at their midpoint, so that the maximum rate of growth is the same for all subprocesses. Such a rule has a defensible interpretation in product sales, because it reflects the stability of consumer spending. People's average income (gross national product) does not change rapidly with time; therefore the buying power of individuals of a certain income class also remains roughly stable over a period of time. As products come and go, rapidly substituting for one another, the maximum rate of product sales does not change appreciably on the average; and the larger the product niche, the longer its life cycle. As a consequence, life cycles become longer during the high-growth period and shorter during the low-growth period, as depicted in Fig. 4-2.

The large S-curve that becomes visible when we zoom backward serves as an envelope for the succession of the smaller constituent curves. Its level defines the ceiling up to which constituents will grow and its steepness determines the length of their life cycle. The phenomenon of shrinking life

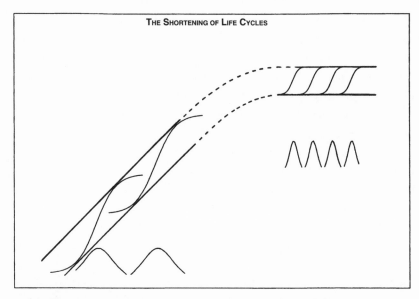

THE SHORTENING OF LIFE CYCLES

FIGURE 4-2. A geometric explanation of why the end of growth implies shorter life cycles.

cycles, an important concern of today's manufacturers, can thus be quantitatively linked to the saturation of the enveloping process (see Table 4-1). For a family of products, shrinking life cycles reflect how close to exhaustion a technology may be. On a larger scale, shrinking life cycles of families of products (for example, mainframe computers) reflect changing social patterns (such as demand for more portable and personalized products). On an even larger scale, a large number of families of products—technologies, markets, and so on—with shrinking life cycles may reflect a global economic recession.

Because the decomposition of the envelope S-curve to the constituent product S-curves has been quantitative, we can relate the shortening of product life cycles to the overall level of saturation—how close it is to exhaustion—of the envelope. We can then monitor the drift of the width of life cycles over time to determine either how close we are to full

TABLE 4-1. The Relation between the
Shortening of Life Cycles and Saturation

LIFE-CYCLE LENGTH (RELATIVE TO LONGEST)	LEVEL OF SATURATION (PERCENT OF CEILING)
0.17	3.1
0.19	4.0
0.20	5.2
0.22	6.9
0.24	9.1
0.30	12.8
0.41	20.0
0.70	31.4
1.00	50.0
0.70	68.6
0.41	80.0
0.30	87.2
0.24	90.9
0.22	93.1
0.20	94.8
0.19	96.0
0.17	96.9

saturation (life cycles getting shorter) or how far we are from a future maximal rate of growth (life cycles getting longer).

In practice, because of technical or other reasons such as pent-up demand, the first few short-lived S-curves in a long chain are often either understated or missing.

EXAMPLES FROM INDUSTRY

DEC became successful thanks to the minicomputer, a market niche created and filled by DEC. The first technology of minicomputers, called PDP, was launched in 1959. In 1978

DEC launched a second architecture of minicomputers, called VAX, based on a 32-bit microprocessor. They replaced half the PDP sales by the mid-1980s. By 1990 DEC launched yet another architecture of computers, called Alpha, based on a 64-bit microprocessor. They replaced half the VAX sales by the mid-1990s. Each architecture had many product families, and each family many products.

As a strategy consultant at DEC, I studied one family of products in detail, the MicroVAXes. They occupied the $20,000 to $50,000 price range. The MicroVAX family is a classical example of one overall S-curve composed of many constituent S-curves. The family's first entrant was MicroVAX I. It had a short life cycle, and it was generally considered an unsuccessful product—unfairly so. It should have been seen as an exploratory attempt that paved the way for the products that followed. MicroVAX II had the longest life cycle—three times as long as its predecessor. The life-cycle duration was already decreasing with the follow-up product, M2000, which lasted for a little more than half as long as MicroVAX II. Later models appeared in rapid succession and featured life cycles more than four times shorter than that of MicroVAX II. According to Table 4-1, this product family should have been around 90 percent exhausted at the time of the study. I was able to obtain a confirmation of this conclusion (87 percent of the level of the ceiling) by constructing the overall curve of the family as a single product. Soon afterward, this price range was taken over by workstations and servers.[9]

Zooming back, we see that the VAX architecture had many product families like MicroVAX. Zooming back further, we see the PDP, VAX, and Alpha technologies all behaving like single products inside DEC's overall company curve. In fact, the life cycles of these architectures are getting shorter. If the life cycle of PDP is taken as unity, the life cycle of VAX is equal to 0.65, which, according to Table

4-1, corresponds to 70 percent completion of the company curve. It also implies that the Alpha architecture will have a life cycle equal to less than 0.4, and therefore should be 50 percent replaced, by something else, around the year 2002. By that time DEC as a company will be at the 85 percent completion level of its overall curve.

Another example of nested S-curves is found in the aviation industry. Wide-body aircraft constitute a family with about a dozen members, each having its own life cycle. Early members, such as the DC10 and Lockheed Tristar, were shorter-lived than the Boeing 747. However, the recent rapid appearance of the 767s, a number of airbuses, MD11s, and 777s implies that these aircraft will have shorter life cycles than the 747s. As in the pattern of Fig. 4-1, the wide-body family of aircraft underwent successive stages: two short life cycles, one long, and again a number of short ones. We can thus conclude that the overall S-curve, describing the growth process of the wide-body family, is approaching a ceiling, with the 747 as the central long-lived product. In the future, we should expect little—if any—growth in the annual passenger-mile totals of wide-body aircraft. In fact, the average size of airliners on transatlantic flights has already shown signs of decline during the mid-1990s. In that light, the superjumbos planned by both Boeing and Airbus have no market. These aircraft, if ever commissioned, would have to steal market share from the wide bodies in use. Even then their sales would never reach the volume of 1400 units anticipated by Airbus managers, or the 500 units estimated by Boeing managers.

We can zoom back and look at all of jet aviation as one family with two members. The first one—early jets—underwent a 15-year growth process. The second one—wide bodies—underwent a 30-year growth process. The picture suggests that there should be an upcoming type of aircraft—possibly supersonic—with relatively high carrying capacity but narrower fuselage (single corridors) than today's wide bodies. The Concorde could be this family's first "unsuccessful" entrant.

Because the life cycles of jet aircraft families have so far been increasing, we conclude that the overall diffusion in jet aviation has not yet passed the midpoint of its S-curve. An independent estimate positions the midpoint of this diffusion process early in the next century.[10] We can thus safely surmise that a new family of supersonic aircraft will grow for longer than 30 years and will constitute the central long-lived family in jet aviation.

SHOWING OFF AT THE DOCK

Being able to estimate the level of overall saturation from observing life-cycle trends is a powerful approach. It implies that a nonspecialist, such as a dock worker loading boxes onto trucks, may notice that the labels on the boxes change three times as frequently as they used to back in the good old days, and boast to his fellow workers that he *knows* that the technology behind these products is more than 87 percent exhausted. He may go further and argue that if things have been done right, the next-technology products should be showing up at the dock with the coming shipment.

This image may sound naive, but the approach offers valuable insights for tracking the overall life cycle of products, families of technologies, and social trends. Examining the evolution of the subprocesses can give us information about the remaining growth potential of the outer envelope. In other words, the shortening of product life cycles tells about the remaining growth potential of the product family. The shortening of product-family life cycles tells about the remaining growth potential of the company. The life cycles of companies tell about the remaining growth potential of the industry, and the life cycles of industries tell about the whole economy.

WHEN DO WE STOP BEING CHILDREN?

We have generalized the decomposition of an overall growth process into finer-grained S-shaped sections, according to the mathematical tradition of Fourier analysis. A Fourier analysis is the decomposition of *any* function into a sum of sines and cosines of different periods. The most slowly varying component—responsible for the main trend—is referred to as the *fundamental harmonic*. In our case, instead of sines and cosines, we decompose *any* growth pattern into S-curves. As with Fourier analysis, we may find that one component plays a major role, even if the overall pattern shows significant deviations from a typical S-curve. By analogy we should say that this is the fundamental harmonic of the growth process and that higher harmonics are expected to play less important roles.

The growth in the size of humans from embryo to adulthood can be analyzed in terms of constituent S-shaped subprocesses.[11] The fundamental harmonic is childhood, extending from 2 to 12 years of age. This period contributes the largest-size chunk to human height and covers more than 90 percent of the total growth period. Second in importance is the growth of the fetus and baby, extending from the period of gestation to some time beyond the age of 1. Adolescence plays a relatively minor role in the acquisition of height, particularly for girls. For boys, it begins at age 13, ends at 19, and contributes only 10 percent to total height. A more in-depth study may discern a finer S-shaped growth process around the egg and the embryo states. Finally, there must be a relatively small downward pointing S-curve describing the shrinking of height with age.

The conclusion of this exercise is that everyday terms such as fetus, baby, child, and adolescent have precise definitions reflecting growth processes that are distinct. There is also an unexpected insight. One and the same S-curve is sufficient to describe both states of fetus and babyhood, as if they belonged to the *same* growth process. This must be related to the fact that the distinction between gestation and babyhood is largely a "geographical" one, meaning inside or outside the womb. After all, the transition between them takes place abruptly, the ratio of the durations between these two stages may vary as much as a factor of 3 from case to case, and the exact time of transition is most often arbitrary (induced labor).

THE END OF THE INFORMATION TECHNOLOGY INDUSTRY

The information technology industry—centered on hardware—entered the final phase of its growth cycle in the early 1990s. The phasing-out implies that its rate of growth will eventually go to zero and that some other industry may be "launched" in replacement. The best candidate for such an industry is what Peter Drucker calls *knowledge technology,* meaning networks, software, knowledge bases, and services all linked via computers, preferably portable ones. In that sense, the computer's role shifts from a main player giving rise to an industry to a simple component in a much larger infrastructure. There is hard evidence that by the mid-1990s the computer industry reached maturity and that in certain key ways, such as the trends in downsizing and in the prices of personal computers, no more surprises should be expected.

NO MORE DOWNSIZING IN COMPUTERS

Computers, like other products, have a revenue distribution that sharply peaks at the low end. As the system's price increases, the revenue in a fixed price band decreases. Price elasticity is reflected in the detailed shape of this distribution—namely, how much the sales volume goes up as the price goes down. (See Appendix B for mathematical descriptions.)

Such a determination of price elasticity is pragmatic as opposed to academic. All marketers' actions and customers' reactions have been de facto taken into account, because the shape of the revenue from *incurred* sales generates the dependence on the price.

By tracking the price elasticity between 1985 and 1995, we find that during the early 1990s elasticity increased significantly, making computers look more and more like commodity products, which are typically characterized by high elasticity. This process, which followed a natural growth curve, practically reached a ceiling in 1993. Price elasticity did not increase for the following 2 years. Computers did not become more commoditylike. But how is this to be reconciled by the popular notion that mainframes are on an extinction course and the fact that increasingly smaller and cheaper machines keep appearing in the market?

There is a twofold answer. Downsizing has also been evident in the trend of the median price, the system price below which half the volume of the whole market is found. The median price has dropped by almost 100-fold since 1986. But just like price elasticity, the median price has also roughly stabilized since 1994. Whereas computers extend into the product range of smaller and cheaper systems, the upper limit on system prices has been moving toward higher prices, largely compensating for the downward drift. In 1993, mainframes carried price tags higher than ever before. The top price for systems sold—as reported by Dataquest 1994—shifted upward from $14.8 million in 1986 (Cray) to $32.5 million (IBM) in 1993. Ten percent of the revenue from computer sales in the U.S. market still came from systems above $3.3 million in 1993.

The moral of the story is that mainframes have reached the end of their extinction course. The tug-of-war between mainframes and client-server systems has entered a stable phase. This does not mean that smaller and more powerful computers will not continue to appear on the market. The low end will most likely continue to amaze us with ever-increasing capabilities for ever-decreasing prices. Lower-price computer systems may enter the marketplace—for example, the network computer (NC)—but the overall revenue distribution from computer sales will not become *any steeper*. The appearance of the new low-price contenders will be at the expense of *all* existing systems, not only the high-end models and mainframes. There is corroborating evidence for this trend.

PERSONAL COMPUTERS ARE NOT GETTING CHEAPER

The actual revenue distribution across the full product range from computer sales shows a "bump" of revenue coming from personal computers. This bump peaked around $3700 in 1985 but evolved in a smooth way and stabilized around $2700 by 1993. Once again, the process traced out a natural S-shaped pattern and reached a plateau. Personal computers continue to become more powerful and acquire increasingly impressive new features. It may look as if they are getting cheaper. Not true! As with cars and other products of mature industries, performance keeps increasing, but prices have found their homeostatic level (equilibrium) and will move further only to account for inflation. From now on, you are expected to spend a stable fraction of your income for your PC, independently of the marvels it will bring you.

The two stabilizing indicators discussed above provide hard evidence that the computer industry entered a winter season during the mid-1990s. This is the period when one growth process comes to an end, while the follow-up process is not yet visible. The four-seasons metaphor implies that the low-growth period and high-growth period are comparable in duration. Computer planners can look forward to several relatively quiet years. But this period brews future surprises. If events have followed their natural course, the new growth trends have already been sown. The role of a personal computer may drift significantly with time; for example, I already use my computer instead of my stereo system. A different kind of PC could enjoy new growth in sales.

To obtain a big picture, we need to extend in time, both in the future and the past. Long-history data and distant future horizons, coupled with natural growth fractals—S-curves nested like Russian dolls—yield rare insights. Substitutions of products and successions of growth phases are cyclical, but the periods drift slowly because the envelope itself goes through a cycle. Moreover, phenomena of different time frames are superimposed. Consequently, we will never come back to quite the same situation. The return of long-range planning activities in a big way during the early twenty-first century will not be similar to that of the 1960s, for several reasons. One such reason is the development of mature cross-disciplinary techniques—for example, chaos models—that were still at conception level in the 1960s.

Positive myopia is a good strategy framework for perhaps 80 percent of the time. The bigger picture provides the remaining 20 percent. The respective efforts required are not at the same ratio, however. The former is a simple recipe, whereas the latter involves natural laws and data analysis.

The Swiss have a saying, "The last 10 percent of a project claims 90 percent of the effort." The ancient Greeks argued that a project's beginning constitutes half its completion. Putting these two together, leaves us with 140 percent of the effort, only for the beginning and the finish of a project.

Oh well, these are the merits of cultural diversity.

INSTINCT VERSUS RATIONALE

- When and how much can I trust my instinct?
- How can I assess, measure, and monitor strategic performance?

Wishful thinking is a strategist's worst enemy. Belief projection is the main ingredient of most strategies. Long-range planning sessions often turn into battles of opinion. Shouting matches invariably lead to deadlock. A DEC vice president responsible for strategic alliances once came to me with the following request: "Our high-level negotiations with *Company X* are stuck at the point where their marketers' opinion clashes with our marketers' opinion. Can you provide us with objective, science-based, defensible arguments in support of the future trends we are advocating?" I did. I analyzed historical data, was able to establish trends that obeyed natural laws, and thus made projections that were free of human biases. The negotiations bore fruit.

In the business arena, ambitious and motivated individuals compete fiercely to make a profit. Competitive advantages are sought by any means, generally complying with society's laws, but *always* honoring nature's laws. It is for that reason that the laws we discussed earlier (natural growth in competition and harmonic succession from one business season to the next) offer a reliable platform for building objective decision support tools. The further the future horizon, the more we need systematic guidance in decision making.

ASSESS, MEASURE, AND MONITOR STRATEGIC PERFORMANCE

Strategic management has become overshadowed by a cloud of uncertainty and confusion. Companies that find themselves in a business winter are frustrated, not knowing if and when they will come out of it, while other companies that may look good on paper (profitable, on budget, and with great balance sheets) may suddenly stumble upon a strategic catastrophe and collapse spectacularly and unexpectedly. Strategic performance enjoys success that is seasonal. There are times when effective optimization demands that leaders step back, relinquish power, and delegate decision making.

Strategic performance measurement has not been the object of rigorous study up to now. The profit impact of market strategy (PIMS) database has produced many good observations on strategies that had good results, in general operational terms.[1] But although many tools have been put in place for monitoring the performance and productivity of the middle and lower ranks, CEOs and managing directors are still being measured in a nonsystematic way. Erratic board reviews and stockholder judgment often come too late and, like tidal waves, sweep dynasties away overnight.

We saw in Chap. 2 that each season requires particular behavioral patterns for success. These patterns, combined with understanding time frames and life-cycle positions, offer mechanisms for measuring strategic performance. The approach consists of checking quantitatively to what extent the leadership is in harmony with the "spirit of the times." Furthermore, since many seasonal attributes refer to qualitative or emotional (that is, instinctive) appreciation of the situation, the approach allows us to evaluate a leader's performance in terms of his or her intuitive understanding of the situation.

Sample Questions in the Questionnaire

BUSINESS	INTUITION
Your pricing policy is:	If your division were likened to a play,
a) Cost-based	it would be:
b) Value-based	a) A romance
c) Arbitrary (decadent profits)	b) A comedy
d) Customer-driven (potentially	c) A tragedy
unprofitable)	d) A satire

Here is an example. Let us say that we want to check the strategic performance of a man who is chief executive of a company's manufacturing division. We ask him to answer two multiple-choice questionnaires, one concerning his intuitive understanding and another concerning his business practices. He can mark more than one choice by specifying different weights according to his priorities.

For example, if his pricing is value-based and the CEO likens his division to a tragedy, he is doing something wrong. Either his instinct or his pricing is inappropriate. Tragedy corresponds to the fall season, when the correct pricing policy is cost-based. Value-based pricing schemes are appropriate in spring, which is likened to a romance.

The CEO's answers can then be gauged against a quantitative estimate of the life-cycle position, obtained via another questionnaire on the present and past growth situation of his division. If the position turns out to be halfway between summer and fall, our manager gets 75 percent for intuition and only 25 percent for rationale on the basis of his answers to these two sample questions. The perennial argument of whether instinct or rationale is best for business can thus be answered for a particular individual in a particular situation.

At Growth Dynamics we have built an interactive software tool that uses dozens of questions to probe rationale and instinct.[2] The estimate of the life-cycle position plays a key role in this approach. To enhance the accuracy of our positioning, we often run a work session involving several informed managers of the division—for example, members of the management board.

We have used this approach with a number of high-level executives. Our experience so far has produced one unexpected result. Although it is not possible to establish unquestionably superior performance of instinct over rationale or vice versa, the variance seems to be systematically biased. It appears that emotions are more prone to sporadic wandering away than reason. Specifically, we found that for the number of executives tested, rational and intuitive performance varied, with sometimes one and sometimes the other performing better. But in all cases, the spread among the intuitive questions was larger than the spread among the rational questions. If this result is significant, it means that instinct, even if it is at times more reliable (better average grade), is fundamentally a more crude instrument of judgment. This result corroborates the findings of the modified Boston Consulting Group (BCG) analysis that we carried out at the Eighth Annual Chicago Pricing Conference (see Chap. 2). Namely, pricing as an art may be more desirable but is less under control than pricing as a science.

An evaluation of instinctive versus rational strategic performance is not necessarily a determination of a genetic or lifelong characteristic. Rationale, like instinct, can have good or bad days.

In business schools today increasing attention is paid to the role of instinct and intuition in decision making. The shift comes in reaction to the emphasis given to analytical management science techniques in the 1980s. It is true that the effectiveness of instinct and rationale—like everything else in business—is seasonal. But business schools are out of phase! The 1990s generally represent a worldwide economic winter. Instinct performs well in summer seasons, when growth processes are well established and their momentum indicates the preferred direction. When you find yourself halfway through a growth process, your instinct has been "educated" during the first half and performs well during the second half. In a winter season, the new direction of growth has not been established yet, and your instinct has not accumulated any experience that way. Winters can benefit more from rationally driven decisions.

Of course, some individuals have more of an instinctive gift than others, and some situations call for more intuition than thinking. Thus it is useful to monitor the performance of your instinct and your rationale from case to case and from time to time. Decision support tools are particularly helpful during stressful times, when instinct may be affected more than intellect and the need for objectivity becomes more crucial.

COULD YOU TAKE AIM AT AN APPLE ON YOUR SON'S HEAD?

Successful businesspeople, especially those making headlines, take pride in claiming that "it is all in the guts." They rarely admit the value in the know-how transmitted through an MBA. Successful entrepreneurs have never been heard to give credit to their university professors as many renowned professionals in the arts and sciences do. Most often credit for business success goes to some popular, folkloric, street-wise education gained outside schools or to some genetic heritage.

Instinctive performance can carry managers a long way, particularly during prosperous times when conditions permit one to "dance" ones way through good business decisions. The difficulties show up during economic recessions when markets start saturating, competition becomes cut-throat, and the game changes from prosperity to survival. As in the performances of musicians and acrobats, heavy psychological stress results in insecurity, panic, and mistakes. William Tell may have been the rare exception, daring to take aim at the apple on his son's head. Most good archers would tremble too much under the stress of what was at stake.

Stress is quite evident among executives who claim, "We had no difficulty positioning our products back when business was booming, but now the issue has acquired crucial importance. How can we be sure we are not making a mistake?" They are simply expressing their need for systematic guidelines in order to continue doing what they have been doing, apparently by instinct. Are there such guidelines? How are they obtained?

Averaging the opinion of experts is one frequently used technique. The exercise can be greatly improved with interactive software tools, such as the modified BCG graph described in Chap. 2. But the process remains subject to collective biases, inasmuch as the experts all belong to the same company or industry (unavoidable if they are supposed to be experts). There is another way to quantify the learning from past successful decisions. The example presented below describes a proven technique to position new computer products and to deal with corrective actions following unexpected delivery delays.[3]

LEARNING FROM EXPERIENCE IN POSITIONING NEW COMPUTER PRODUCTS

The concept of competition can be generalized beyond products. Means of transportation are found to compete for passengers, just as primary energy sources compete for consumers. Carrying this thinking further, we can see criminal organizations competing with the police force and even diseases competing for victims.[4] Finally, every learning process involves competition as "things" compete for our attention. The learning curves used in psychology and sociology are all S-shaped. The accumulation of learning, depicted by an S-curve, does not always refer to a person. It may be a group of people, an organization, or humanity as a whole that learns. Below we consider the learning accumulated by the engineers designing computers at a large computer manufacturer.

The performance of a computer is gauged by its speed—for example, how many millions of instructions per second (MIPS) it can execute. For a long time the figure of merit for a computer model—its value—was represented by the ratio of performance to price, expressed in MIPS/$. I studied DEC's VAX family products from the very first model to the mainframes launched in 1990. DEC's research engineers—like those of other companies—had been creating increasingly powerful computers for less money. The MIPS/$ ratio for all VAXes followed S-shaped curves. By studying all successful products up to that time, I was able to produce a set of learning curves, one for each major family of products. These curves represented the learning accumulated by the community of the company's engineers. In 1990, this learning process was still young, because the data occupied in general only the early exponential part of the curves. Consequently, estimates of the final ceiling carried large uncertainties (up to 100 percent). Our knowledge, however, of a level for this ceiling was so poor that even very uncertain estimates were welcome.

It was interesting, for example, to find out that we had a long way to go. This may sound like a trivial conclusion, but thanks to the way it was obtained, it said more than simply "humans will always make progress." It said that a certain amount of computer evolution was guaranteed by the fundamental technologies available. Breakthroughs would certainly keep coming along. Nothing as dramatic as the discovery of the transistor, however, would be warranted in order to reach three to four times the levels of performance/price. Of course, the appearance of an earthshaking breakthrough, a discovery of importance unprecedented during computer history, could define a much higher ceiling, to be reached through follow-up curves.

There were other benefits from fitting an S-shaped curve to sales data points. The mathematical description of this curve—the logistic-growth function—relates price and performance with time in a quantitative way. Specifying two of these variables dictates a value for the third one. The most obvious place to use such a result is in pricing a new product. Its performance (MIPS for computers) is known and not easy to change. For a chosen introduction date, the function determines the MIPS/$ ratio, which yields a price value.

The first time we used this method at DEC for guidance in positioning new products, we were also confronted with the introduction of a new technology: RISC (reduced instruction set computing). DEC had two new powerful workstations to price, one of the traditional architecture and one of RISC architecture.

Recommending a price for the traditional system was

straightforward. The new-technology product, however, posed several problems. First, the variable MIPS/$ was no longer "kosher." MIPS in the traditional environment is not the same as MIPS in the RISC environment. Moreover, the experts would not be unanimous about the equivalence of the two environments. Even worse, RISC was significantly more important than previous technological improvements. Would RISC follow the same learning curves or would it create its own with different parameters?

The experts were assembled for brainstorming. In addition to their opinion on the equivalence of MIPS, I wanted their opinion on the following question: "How different is the new technology from the old one?" To quantify their answers, I had a follow-up question: "Is it as different as passing from vacuum-tube amplifiers to transistors?"

This time the experts were unanimous. RISC was a technology *very* different from the old technology, but *not as different* as transistors were from tubes. From then on it was a question of judgment. For lack of other guidelines, my final recommendation was to put RISC on the S-curve representing the low-end of the product range. A few quarters later, the market price of both products settled very close to the recommended values.

During my experience with DEC computers I came across occasional exceptions. Some products would not fall on a curve. For example one product—MicroVAX II—was significantly at the left of the curve representing the low-end product range. This could mean a number of things:

- The product was announced 6 months too early.
- The product was too powerful by 15 percent.
- The product was underpriced by 15 percent.
- The product was positioned to gain market share.

The truth is that the product was indeed positioned to gain market share.

Another product—Ft 3000—fell significantly on the right of the curve representing the high-end of the product range, as if it came to market 6 months too late, was underperforming, or was overpriced. In truth, the product was a heavily redundant system designed to be fault-tolerant for special critical applications; it was therefore priced accordingly.

These guidelines for product positioning are obtained from data on successful products. By following them we can aspire to reduce errors resulting from a stressful environment and to continue being successful.

In addition to price setting, the results of such a study provide a means for deciding on corrective actions following delays in product delivery. Product announcements precede shipments by a variable amount of time. More than for reasons of inflation, products coming to market late are worth less. How much should a price be dropped following an unexpected delay? Alternatively, how much should the performance be improved if we insist upon keeping the same price?

With the growth function determined, mathematical manipulations (partial time derivatives) can provide answers to these questions. For the first case, adjusting the price for unexpected delays, we find that the adjustment following a quarter's delay should decrease exponentially with time. In other words, delivery delays hurt most at the time of introduction. Later on, further delays cost less. This result should not surprise businesspeople.

What may come as a surprise is the second case, improving performance in order to keep the same price. The performance enhancements required by a quarter's delay go through a bell-shaped evolution. As shipments are delayed, the performance must be increased. The increase is larger every year as the product approaches the middle of the learning curve, which for DEC's low-end computers fell around 1995. From then onward, however, the product would require less and less improvement in its performance for comparable delays. This is because the MIPS/$ growth curve in question began to flatten out after 1995. Consequently a slippage in delivery would require a smaller improvement in performance than it would have previously.

THE INDUSTRY LEARNING CURVE

Most industrial knowledge has been acquired on the job. As a consequence, such knowledge is characterized not only by unquestionable validity but also by a lack of analytical formulation. Unquestionable truths are intriguing because they signal an underlying law. In my search for guidelines for successful business decisions, I found that mathematical manipulations of the S-curve equation yield pairs of relationships between price and time, performance and time, or price and performance. While I was carrying out those manipulations I stumbled onto a new derivation for a fundamental piece of industrial knowledge: the economies of scale.

Economies of scale mean that the more units you produce of a product, the less each unit costs to produce. Production costs decrease with volume for a variety of reasons: automation, sharing overhead, reducing material costs through wholesale prices, and general process optimization resulting from production experience. A major part of the cost reduction can be attributed to *learning* in some way or another.

Business schools teach economies of scale qualitatively by the *volume curve*, which shows that costs per unit decrease as a function of the volume of units produced. The theoretical argument is that costs are typically proportional to the area (surface) of whatever is being produced and consequently increase more slowly than the volume. The curve looks like a hyperbola, or a decreasing exponential, reaching a minimum final value when the costs can be reduced no further. But this kind of curve could be our familiar S-curve in disguise!

The mathematical expression of the S-curve is the logistic-growth function. This function is a simple fraction that has a constant in the numerator and a constant plus a decreasing exponential in the denominator (see Appendix B). It is exactly the inverse of an economies-of-scale expression (costs per unit being equal to a constant plus an exponential). In other words, the volume curve can be well approximated by the inverse of the S-shaped learning curve. Businesspeople using volume curves for decades may have been dealing with S-curves without realizing it. The moral of the story is that learning alone can account for the reduction of costs with volume.

The truth probably involves both phenomena: learning *and* the fact that costs increase like a surface—that is, slower than the volume. But I am convinced that learning will play a progressively important role. In the manufacturing of microprocessors, for example, the surface-to-volume argument for the definition of costs breaks down. The argument will break down further with such future pillars of the world economy as services, telecommunications, and the Internet. Learning is fundamental because it is linked to natural growth in competition.

LIFE CYCLES OF SERVICES

In 1989 I presented a paper to an international conference on "Diffusion of Technologies and Social Behavior" at IIASA, in Laxemburg, Austria.[5] The topic of my paper was a quantitative determination of the service life cycle of computers. I was proud to make that presentation for two reasons. One reason was that, to formulate the technique, I had put into practice an "exotic" mathematical procedure called convolution of functions, which up to that time had been a purely academic exercise for me. The other reason was that we had saved millions of dollars in service revenue at DEC by using the service life-cycle technique. Pressure had been mounting in the company to stop manufacturing spare parts for the very first VAX minicomputer—the VAX 11/780—which had finished its sales life cycle many years ago. By showing that 30 percent of the service revenue for this product was still to come, we helped convince manufacturing to continue producing the parts necessary for the computer's maintenance.

During my presentation, someone in the audience pointed out that a recent article in the *Harvard Business Review* treated the same subject. Alarmed, I rushed to obtain a copy of that issue. Indeed, the article showed similar curves to the ones I produced by convoluting S-curves.[6] But the discussion was purely qualitative. There was no way to estimate a product's position on the curve or the time frame and remaining growth potential for the service revenue.

I doubt that DEC would have saved money by circulating that article in the manufacturing division.

GENETIC REENGINEERING OF CORPORATIONS

- How can our role in the market become more predator and less prey?
- Should we go for differentiation or for counter-attack?
- Is our advertising budget spent in the most productive way? Do we need to change our image?

The S-shaped curve describes the growth in competition of a species population. Competition results because members of the same species elbow one another in a crowded niche. In the presence of more than one species, the S-curve law does not generally apply, because one species can interfere with the growth rate of another in many ways. More terms must be added to the mathematical formulation to take this interaction into account, and the S-shape pattern becomes distorted. An exception is one-to-one substitutions: They involve two competitors only, and yet their "market" shares follow S-shaped patterns (see the case of cars and horses discussed in Chap. 1).

There are two bends in the graceful shape of the celebrated S-curve. The first one (exponential rise) is due to the capability of the species to multiply. The second one (niche-saturation slowdown) is due to the competitive squeeze caused by the limited space.

THE FIRST BEND.   If you put a pair of rabbits on a fenced-off range, you can watch their population increase by the successive stages of 2, 4, 8, 16, 32,..., 2^n, in an exponential growth. If the average rabbit litter is greater than 2, you will see a steeper exponential growth. The same is true with products, because they too can multiply. Depending upon its attractiveness—the equivalent of the average rabbit litter—every product sold will bring new customers. The more products out there and the more attractive they are, the higher the rate of sales. Sales will grow at a constant percent rate—that is, exponentially—for a while, with a time constant defined by product attractiveness. (If a product's attractiveness is smaller than unity, each product sold will bring less than one new customer, indicating that we are dealing with an unsuccessful entry, and its sales will quickly dwindle to zero.)

THE SECOND BEND.   The rabbit population explosion ceases when a sizable part of the niche becomes occupied; the same is true with products. The growth equation that is valid for late *as well as* early times contains a second factor: the fact that the niche capacity is finite (see Appendix A). In other words, the equation says that the percentage rate of growth is proportional not only to product attractiveness but also to the still-empty space in the market niche.

MORE THAN ONE SPECIES IN THE SAME NICHE

Two parameters, attractiveness and niche capacity, fully determine the S-shaped pattern arising from a species population diffusing in its ecological niche. But what happens if besides rabbits we have sheep on the range? After all, sheep also eat grass and in greater amounts than rabbits. Their presence will certainly suppress the rabbit population explosion. Worse yet, what happens if there are foxes? Competition between rabbits and sheep is not the same as between rabbits and foxes. Just think of the fact that, faced with a finite amount of grass, sheep would probably lament at the rapid multiplication of rabbits, whereas foxes would undoubtedly rejoice.

The basic mechanism is how one competitor influences the growth rate of the other. Sheep and rabbits have a negative effect on each other's population by reducing each other's food supply. In contrast, foxes damage rabbit populations, while rabbits enhance fox populations. Whenever there is more than one competitor in the same niche, we must consider the interaction between them—namely, how one's rate of growth depends on the existence of the other. We then need to introduce a third parameter in the growth equation to take this coupling into account. The value of this parameter is related to the overlap between competitors, or how much one steps on the other's feet—in other words, how many sales we will lose (or win) because our competitor won one. This way we can formulate a measurement for our ability to attack, counterattack, or retreat, as the case may be.

ATTACKER'S ADVANTAGE, DEFENDER'S COUNTERATTACK

The attack of a new species against the defenses of an incumbent lies at the heart of corporate marketing strategies. This kind of struggle has already been rigorously formulated by biologists and ecologists. In the 1930s George Gause, at Moscow's Zoological Museum, studied the competition between a traditional brewer's yeast and one used in the Ukraine to make the refreshing milk drink called *kefir*, popular in Asian and Middle Eastern countries. He first grew the two yeasts in isolation and observed the S-shaped natural growth pattern for each. He then put them together in the same test tube and let them compete for the same food. He found that each influenced the other's growth. But the brewer's yeast is tolerant to the alcohol that is produced as it grows; the kefir yeast is less so. In a mixture, the brewer's yeast thus had an increasing advantage as fermentation proceeded, and it outgrew its competitor. Simple S-shaped curves did not describe the growth processes well because they could not handle the interference of the growth rate of one on the other. But the Volterra-Lotka mathematical formulation involves coupling constants and can do that.

Christopher Farrell, director of scientific affairs at Baxter Healthcare, defines an *attacker's advantage* and a *defender's counterattack* in terms of the coupling parameters in the growth equations.[1] The attacker's advantage quantifies the extent to which the attacker inhibits the ability of the defender to keep market share. The defender's counterattack quantifies the extent to which the defender can prevent the attacker from stealing market share. The business strategy and tactics of attack and counterattack have been qualitatively described by Peter Drucker (1985) and especially by Richard Foster (1986), director at McKinsey & Co. The nature of the attacker's advantage has been clearly established by Cooper and Kleinschmidt (1990)—professors respectively in industrial marketing and technology management and in marketing and international business—who studied over 200 new products and determined that the most significant parameter in gaining market share is a "superior product that delivered unique benefits to the user." This and price considerations dictate the magnitude of the attacker's advantage.

Under attack, the defender redoubles its own efforts to maintain or improve its position. A high value for the defender's counterattack implies a face-on counterattack within the context "we do better what they do." An effective counterattack, however, with long-lasting survival-sustaining consequences implies eventual adoption of the new technology and some sort of death for the old company, an end that is painful to assimilate culturally. Because companies hesitate to embark on such undertakings, Foster refers to the defender's counterattack as the defender's *dilemma* and cites tens of examples in which a defender refused to acknowledge, or reacted too late, to an attacker's onslaught. A classical case was NCR's belated and traumatic transition to computerized cash registers.

Figure 6-1 shows a more recent example, the competi-

MOBILE-TELEPHONE SALES IN GREECE

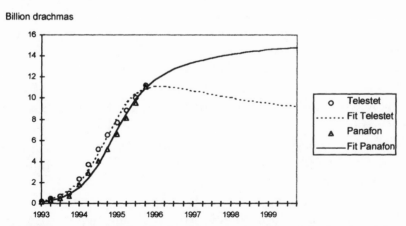

FIGURE 6-1.   Quarterly sales for the two competitors of the Greek mobile-telephone market. Despite early dominance by Telestet, the model successfully predicted the shift in Panafon's favor by mid-1996.

tion in the Greek mobile-telephone market, a two-competitor struggle. Panafon and Telestet launched their products simultaneously. Telestet became an early market leader, thus assuming the role of defender. But the coupling parameters, determined from the data, were both negative and significant: the attacker's advantage $= -0.8$ and the defender's counterattack $= -0.6$. The figures indicated much overlap and fierce competition of the sheep-rabbit nature. Every time Panafon would close a sale, Telestet would lose 0.8 potential sales, and every time Telestet would close a sale, Panafon would lose 0.6 sales. The difference was crucial. The model showed curves that eventually deviated from S-shapes. With data up to the end of 1995, the model's prediction was that Panafon would become leader within a few months. By mid-1996 Panafon's market share was indeed higher than Telestet's.

Kristina Smitalova and Stefan Sujan—professors of mathematics at Comenius University and the Slovac Academy of Science respectively, in Bratislava, Slovakia—studied and classified the various coupling schemes rigorously.[2] They distinguished and labeled six ways in which two competitors can influence each other's growth rate, according to the sign of the two coupling parameters involved. The tabulations are shown in the boxed text.

Pure competition is what occurs between rabbits and sheep. Each one diminishes the growth of the other but not with the same importance (sheep are fewer but eat more). Market examples are the mobile-telephone case mentioned above and the competition between different-size computer models.

Predator-prey is the case of cinema and television. The more movies made for cinema, the more television will benefit, but the more television grows in importance, the more cinema suffers. Films made for TV are not shown in movie

> $--$ *Pure competition* occurs when both species suffer from each other's existence.
>
> $+-$ *Predator-prey* occurs when one species serves as direct food to the other.
>
> $++$ *Mutualism* occurs in the case of symbiosis, or a win-win situation.
>
> $+0$ *Commensalism* occurs in a parasitic type of relationship in which one species benefits from the existence of the other, which nevertheless remains unaffected.
>
> -0 *Amensalism* occurs when one species suffers from the existence of the other, which is impervious to what is happening.
>
> 00 *Neutralism* occurs if there is no interaction whatsoever.

theaters. Had there been no legal protection (restricting permission to broadcast new movies), television would have probably "eaten up" the cinema audience.

A typical case of mutualism is software and hardware. Sales of each trigger more sales for the other.

Add-ons and accessories such as car extras illustrate commensalism. The more cars sold, the more car accessories will be sold. The inverse is not true, however; sales of accessories do not trigger car sales.

Amensalism can be found with ballpoint pens and fountain pens, described in detail below. The onslaught of ballpoint sales seriously damaged fountain pen sales, yet the ballpoint pen population grew as if there were no competition.

Neutralism arises in all situations in which there is no market overlap—for example, a sports store that sells both swimming wear and ski wear. Depending on the geography there might be a negative correlation of seasonal origin, but the sales of one product do not in general affect the sales of the other.

COMPETITION MANAGEMENT

The intriguing fascination of the marketplace is that the *nature* of competition can be changed over time. For some businesspeople, achieving a change in the competitive roles is perhaps more handsomely rewarding than making profits. It is something that species in nature cannot do. Rabbits will never eat meat, and whenever humans tamper in such areas, either academically (genetic engineering) or industrially (mad cow disease), they are invariably criticized, justly or unjustly.

But things are different in industry. In contrast to the jungle, a technology, a company, or a product does not need to remain prey to another forever. The competitive roles can be radically altered with the right decisions at the right time. External light meters, used for accurate diaphragm and speed setting on photographic cameras, enjoyed a stable *commensal* relationship with cameras for decades. As camera sales grew, so did the sales of light meters. But eventually technological developments enabled cameras to incorporate light meters into their own box. Soon the whole light-meter industry became prey to the camera industry. Sales of external light meters diminished while sales of cameras enjoyed a boost, and the relationship passed from *commensalism* to *predator-prey*.

The struggle between fountain pens and ballpoint pens, mentioned earlier, had a happier ending. Another case of genetic reengineering in the marketplace, the substitution of ballpoint pens for fountain pens as writing instruments went through three distinct stages.

Before the appearance of ballpoint pens, fountain pen sales were growing undisturbed to fill the writing instrument market. They were following an S-shaped "rabbit curve" when the ballpoint technology made its appearance in 1951. As ballpoint sales picked up, those of fountain pens declined for the period 1951 to 1973. Ballpoint pens did not belong to the same species or even constitute a one-to-one substitution, yet they cut deeply into fountain pen sales. A simple S-shaped pattern could not have described this transition, but the Volterra-Lotka equations did, with attacker's advantage $= -0.5$ and defender's counterattack $= 0$ (see Fig. 6-2).[3] These numbers imply a competitive advantage for ballpoint pens, which by winning one customer inflict losses of half a customer to fountain pens. Fountain pens staged a counterattack by radically dropping prices for many years. Their

THE STRUGGLE BETWEEN BALLPOINT AND FOUNTAIN PENS

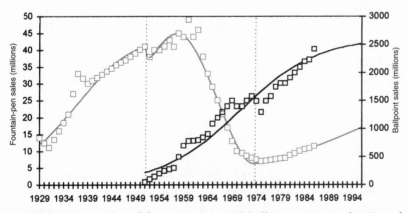

FIGURE 6-2. Sales of fountain pens and ballpoint pens in the United States. The lines are our model's descriptions. Before 1951 and after 1973 we see *plain* S-shaped patterns for each competitor. Between 1951 and 1974 we see a typical *amensal* type of competition, in which the attacker has an advantage (attacker's advantage = −0.5), and the defender's counterattack is null (defender's counterattack = 0).

average price dipped as low as 72 cents. But the counterattack was ineffective—*defender's counterattack* remained equal to zero. Counterattacking fountain pens lost market share and embarked on a well-established extinction course.

Eventually the prices of fountain pens began rising. The average pen price in the United States reached $3.50 in 1980 and continued rising. In 1988 a Mont Blanc Masterpiece Diplomat retailed at $280, and a Waterman Le Mans 100 Briarwood cost $400. The fountain pen underwent what Darwin would have described as a "character displacement" to the luxury niche of the executive pen. The strategy of fountain pens since the early 1970s has been a retreat into noncompetition. Indeed, the *attacker's advantage* and the *defender's counterattack* must both equal zero for the Volterra-Lotka equations to do justice to the sales data of writing instruments in this period. In other words, we have two species that do not interact—*neutralism*—but each follows a simple S-shaped growth pattern. As a consequence, fountain pens have secured for themselves a healthy and profitable market niche. If they had persisted in their competition with ballpoint pens, they would have perished.

Now that we have quantified the competitive mechanisms from 1951 to 1973, it is amusing to play out the following scenario: What would have happened if fountain pens had undergone their character displacement 5 years earlier? The model's answer is a significantly higher number of sales for fountain pens today. Is it believable?

Arguably so. Fountain pens would have embarked on an upward trajectory earlier, starting from a stronger position. Enhanced fountain pen content in everyday life could have had cultural repercussions over time, producing societal preferences and habits. In the end, a more favorably disposed average citizen could have meant a more important role for fountain pens today. Consequently, on the average, their price would have had to rise less and their image would be a little more popular and a little less exclusive.

Character displacement is a classical way to diminish the impact of competition. Another name for this is *Darwinian divergence,* encountered among siblings. In his book *Born to Rebel,* Frank Sulloway—a historian-of-science turned sociologist at MIT's program in science, technology, and society—proves that throughout history first-born children have become conservative and later-borns revolutionary. First-born children end up conservative because they do not want to lose any of the only-child privileges they enjoy. But this forces later-borns into becoming rebellious, to differentiate themselves and thus minimize competition and optimize survival in the same family.[4]

FINDING THE MAGIC ADVERTISING MESSAGE

The Volterra-Lotka equations require three parameters per competitor to describe growth in a two-competitor niche. One parameter represents the ability to multiply, another the size of the niche, and the third interference from the other competitor. Consequently, there are three choices for action, or six if we want to consider the parameters of the competitor. To increase the prospects for growth then, we can try to change one or more of the following:

• The product attractiveness (increase ours or decrease theirs)

• The size of the market niche (increase ours or decrease theirs)

• The nature of the interaction (increase our attack or decrease their attack)

Each direction of action in principle affects only one parameter.[5] But it is not obvious which change will produce the greater effect; it depends on the particular situation. The concrete actions may include performance improvements, price changes, image transformation, and advertising campaigns. Performance and price concern "our" products only, but advertising via the appropriate message can in principle influence all aspects of competition, producing an effect on all six parameters. The question is how much of an effect a certain effort will produce. Some advertising messages have proved significantly more effective than others. Success is not necessarily a result of whim, chance, or other after-the-fact explanations based on psychological arguments. The roles and positions of the competitors at a given point in time determine which advertising message will be the effective one (Fig. 6-3). The effectiveness of advertising messages can be illustrated by a typical competitive technological substitution: woven carpets and tufted carpets.

Woven carpets were made on a loom in a manner similar to plain cloth, except that extra wrap yarns were introduced and raised by wires to form loops. Most of today's carpets

THE SIX DIMENSIONS OF ADVERTISING ACTION

	Attractiveness	Niche size	Competition
WE:	↗ Our products are good	↗ You need our products	↘ We are different
THEY:	↘ Their products are not good	↘ You do not need their products	↗ We do better what they do

FIGURE 6-3. The six possible independent advertising messages according to our model.

are made with needles that punch loops through a backing and retreat to leave tufts. Examining the backing of a typical modern carpet reveals that glue holds the tufts in place. This revolution in carpet making began in the 1950s. Tufting changed the requirements for the yarn. Long, continuous filaments were preferred, since they didn't pill or fuzz. Wool yarn has fibers as short as the annual growth of a sheep's hair. A fiber such as nylon thus moved into very good position, especially when DuPont invented a bulked form of continuous fiber. The combination of bulking and tufting created a new "species" that satisfied a growing demand for carpeting and caused the displacement of woolen woven carpets by nylon tufted ones.[6]

The model description of the data indicates that the *attacker's advantage* $= -2.2$ and the *defender's counterattack* $= -2.6$. This is a typical situation of *pure competition* between two similar-species contenders even though the attacker sells in greater numbers. The fate of the defender is eventual extinction.

Could the makers of woolen woven carpets have secured for themselves a market niche the way fountain pens did? If so, what line of action might they have followed? Let us explore alternative lines of action—via advertising campaigns—and their effectiveness in shaping a different future for woolen carpets back in 1979. We will rate the different scenarios stemming from changing the six parameters one at a time *by the same amount,* which can be taken as a rough equivalent to comparable-effort investment. It is a sensitivity study on the effectiveness of the corresponding advertising message.

Figure 6-4 shows two of the six possible results.[7] Effective campaigns would be those that emphasized attractiveness and differentiation with messages like "Wool is good" and "Wool is different from nylon." However, a coun-

SUBSTITUTING NYLON-TUFTED CARPETS FOR WOOLEN-WOVEN ONES.

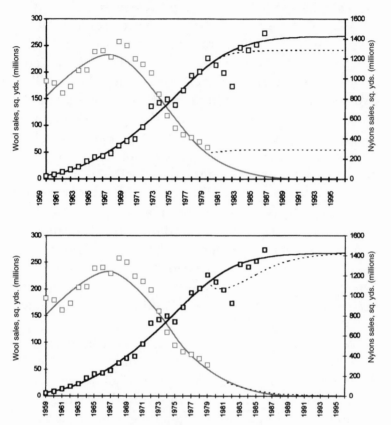

FIGURE 6-4. The dotted lines indicate two scenarios of comparable change in the respective parameters: on the top following an advertising campaign under the slogan "Wool is different from nylon"; on the bottom under the slogan "Wool is better than nylon."

terattack along the lines of "Wool is better than nylon" would have been very ineffective.

Table 6-1 shows the complete list of possible advertising messages and their effect on the evolution of wool and nylon sales in 1979. Each message represents an *indepen-*

TABLE 6-1. Sensitivity Analysis

MESSAGE	EFFECTIVENESS	WOOL	NYLON
Wool is good.	Highest	Slowly rising from '79 level	Little compromised
Wool is different from nylon.	High	Stabilizes at '79 level	Little compromised
You do not need nylon.	Medium	Stabilizes at 0.5 of '79 level	Huge loss of market
Nylon is bad.	Poor	Stabilizes at 0.3 of '79 level	Serious loss of market
Wool is better than nylon.	Negligible	Null	Temporary losses only
You need wool.	Null	No effect	No effect

dent direction in which the full traditional advertising machinery would have to be launched. There should be no crosstalk between directions. For example, to obtain maximum benefit from the "Wool is good" message, a campaign *should not* mix connotations such as "Wool is better than nylon" or "Nylon is bad." Each message would have to be developed and exploited separately.

Although the detailed execution of the advertising campaign (media, wording, style, and so on) remains crucial, the effectiveness ratings of the above directions come in a nonobvious if not surprising order and could not have been arrived at by intuitive or other methods used by advertising agencies. Furthermore, the order may be completely different at another time or in another market.

Table 6-1 shows the results of the complete sensitivity analysis following six scenarios played for the wool-nylon case study. Playing the scenarios from wool's point of view, we measure effectiveness according to how much wool benefits (see Appendix A for the technical details).

Finally, there is a way to assess the size of the advertising investment called for. An advertising campaign along the lines of "Our product is good" affects the product's attractiveness just as a price cut does. (Price can be quantitatively related to attractiveness via price elasticity.) The costs incurred from price dropping alone can thus be compared with those of an advertising campaign that achieved the same result. Naturally, this assessment may result in an overestimate or an underestimate depending on how the advertising campaign in question rated to the "Our product is good" alternative in the sensitivity analysis. It should be noted, however, that if the survival of woolen carpets depended on price dropping alone, the price would have to be cut by more than 100 percent!

The case of the Greek mobile-telephone market, described earlier in Fig. 6-1, is more malleable. As indicated, Telestet could have anticipated its eventual loss of the leading position. If its managers had taken action in the beginning of 1996 toward increasing the attractiveness of its products by 10 percent—for example, by dropping prices 8 percent—Telestet would have safeguarded its lead. Of course, Panafon may have rapidly responded in kind, but this is what the business game is all about—and to a large extent it can be successfully, and painlessly, simulated on your personal computer!

WHO IS AFRAID OF THE BIG BAD WOLF?

The S-curve model enhanced with two-species interactions, as presented above, accounts for the three most fundamental factors that shape growth: the attractiveness of an offering, the size of its market niche, and the interaction with the competition. (When there is more than one competitor, the situation can always be reduced to two players by considering the major competitor only, or by grouping all others together.) Naturally, other factors influence growth, such as channels, distribution, market fragmentation, total market growth, market share, frequency of innovations, productivity in the ranks, and organizational and human resource issues. Many factors can be expressed as combinations of the three fundamental ones. Alternatively, the model could be elaborated—by adding more parameters—to take more phenomena into account.

As it stands, the model provides the baseline, the trend on top of which other, higher-order effects will be superimposed. It guides the strategist through effective genetic manipulations of the competitive roles in the marketplace. It should be used as a front end to what is usually done. The model works equally well for products, corporations, technologies, and whole industries. Only the time frames differ. The pleasure is all the strategist's, who now has a quantitative, science-based way to understand the crux of the competitive dynamics and to anticipate the consequences of possible actions.

Just think—at this very moment there may be a cost-effective way to terminate the state of being prey to the voracious competitor that has been feeding persistently on your achievements.

MAKE THE FUTURE WHAT IT USED TO BE

- What can be predicted? How much choice do I really have and when?
- How can I secure another spring season for my company? For myself?

When I heard the phrase "The future is no longer what it used to be," it produced an echo in me. Unquestionably, life is becoming increasingly unpredictable. The last two decades of the twentieth century have demonstrated relentless change in unexpected directions. The "depression" of the early 1990s—discussed in Chap. 3—will last around 10 years and accentuate uncertainties by nurturing entrepreneurial attitudes. The general trial-and-error search for new directions of economic growth produces a rather fluid and chaotic situation with repercussions in all directions. Back in the 1960s engineering students were told to expect an average of six job offers upon graduation. The difference among the jobs offered was of practically no importance compared with the concerns of students graduating in the 1990s. Their future is no longer the same. The future is no longer the same in terms of predictability. There are too many unknowns, because the well-established, easy-to-forecast growth processes are too few. If we could increase our ability to see into the future, we would recognize familiar patterns in it.

Impressive scientific achievements may prompt us to turn toward science for predicting the future. After all, like business forecasters, scientists develop methods for "telling the future." They merely use a different vocabulary. In contrast to fortune tellers, scientists talk about calculations instead of predictions, laws instead of fate, and statistical fluctuations instead of accidents. Yet the aim of the scientific method is the same. From the observation of past events, scientists derive laws that, when verified, enable them to predict the future.

Classical physics is excellent at describing the movements of billiard balls. The difficulty comes from putting many balls together (many, for physicists, can be anything greater than three). Molecules in a volume of gas behave very much like billiard balls, but there are too many molecules, and they bounce too often. Thermodynamics, the branch of physics that studies gases, makes predictions by focusing on the macroscopic variables only: temperature, pressure, and volume. The bottom-up approach—tracking individual molecules—taxed the ingenuity of the best minds in physics for at least 100 years and has aided only in understanding, corroborating, and justifying the relations established experimentally among the overall variables.

An energy system can be viewed as many microscopic variables (individuals) in random motion. What can be observed is an envelope, such as overall energy consumption for the world, for a nation, or for one particular kind of fuel. To emulate physics, we may be tempted to reconstruct the envelope from the microscopic variables, the individual energy consumers. But this would be as difficult as it is to track billiard balls and gas molecules, and the proof lies with the failed attempts at weather and economic forecasting—because of the vast number of microscopic variables.

A far wiser approach is to concentrate on the macro-

scopic variables that describe the overall behavior of a phenomenon. Cesare Marchetti does just that. He considers
the primary energy consumption worldwide. Figure 7-1
shows the market shares, *in calories,* of each primary energy
source versus time. The fitted S-shaped curves show up as
straight lines as a result of a scale transformation. The fits
are on the historical period 1900 to 1920 only. The curves
are then extrapolated both forward and backward in time.
The agreement between data and lines outside the fitted
region is impressive. Half a century and a world war did not

PREDICTABLE PRIMARY-ENERGY TRENDS

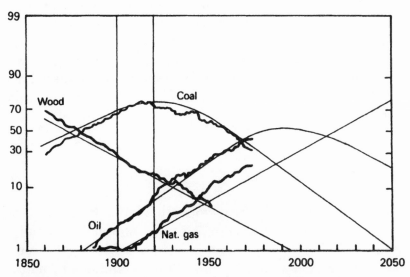

FIGURE 7-1. The irregular lines are the data on world energy consumption
in terms of basic primary energy sources. The smooth lines are S-curves determined from the data of the period 1900 to 1920. The vertical scale is such that
S-curves appear as straight lines. The curved sections reflect the transitional
periods not amenable to S-curve description.

interfere with the natural transition from one energy source to another. The market share of oil in 1970 could have been predicted in 1920 with a precision of 2 to 3 percent. The same is true for coal. The only forecast that did not fit well was that for natural gas. The reason is that the historical window contains the very beginning of the natural gas trajectory, when behavior is particularly unreliable because trends are not well established.[1]

The conclusion is that the present can be used to "unfold" both the future and the past. Information from the present contains the elements essential for this unfolding. If the "present" is a short historical window—some companies keep records for only 2 years—the unfolded future is fuzzy and uncertain. But if the present is a lengthy historical window, like the two decades considered in the above energy example, then the future (and past) image generated is rather sharp. Historical records, combined with an understanding of fundamental processes such as natural growth in competition, can help penetrate the unknown future with improved visibility. But there are natural laws that are even simpler and more fundamental than growth in competition.

INVARIANTS

The simplest possible law dictates that something does not change—a universal constant, or an *invariant* in scientific terms. Invariants are, of course, the easiest things to forecast. They reflect states of equilibrium maintained by natural regulatory mechanisms. In ecosystems such an equilibrium is called *homeostasis* and refers to the harmonious coexistence of predator and prey in a world where species rarely become extinct for natural reasons.

States of equilibrium can also be found in many aspects of social living. Whenever the level of a hardship or a menace increases beyond the tolerable threshold, corrective mechanisms are automatically triggered to lower it. However, if the threat accidentally falls below the tolerated level, society becomes blasé about it, and the corresponding indicators start creeping up again.

Invariants tend to hide behind headlines. For example, the number of deaths from motor vehicle accidents becomes alarming when journalists report statistics for a large country such as the United States over a 3-day weekend. However, when averaged over a year and divided by 100,000 inhabitants, the rate becomes so stable over time and geography that it emerges as rather reassuring!

THE NONSENSE ABOUT SAFE DRIVING

Car safety is a subject of great interest and emotion.[2] Cars have been compared to murder weapons. Each year close to 200,000 people worldwide die from car accidents, and up to 10 times as many may suffer injuries. Efforts are continually made to render cars safer and drivers more cautious. Have such efforts been effective in lowering the death rate? Can this rate be significantly reduced as society becomes more advanced?

To answer those questions, we must look at the history of car accidents. But in order to search for a fundamental law, we must have accurate data and a relevant indicator. Deaths are better recorded and more easily interpreted than less serious accidents. Moreover, the car as a public menace is a threat to society, which may "feel" the dangers and try to keep them under control. Consequently, the number of deaths per 100,000 inhabitants per year becomes a better indicator than accidents per mile, or per car, or per hour of driving.

Figure 7-2 charts data for the United States from the beginning of the century. What we observe is that deaths caused by car accidents grew in a natural way—along an S-shaped pattern—until the mid-1920s, when they reached about 23 per 100,000 per year. From then onward they seem to have stabilized, even though the number of cars continued to grow. A homeostatic mechanism entered into action when this limit was reached, resulting in an oscillating pattern around the equilibrium position. The peaks may have produced public outcries for safety, whereas the valleys could have contributed to the relaxation of speed limits and safety regulations. What is remarkable is that for 65 years there has been a persistent self-regulation of car safety despite tremendous variations in car numbers and performance, speed limits, safety technology, driving legislation, and education.[3]

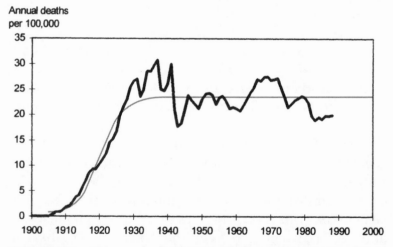

SAFETY IN CARS

Annual deaths
per 100,000

FIGURE 7-2.   The annual number of deaths from motor vehicle accidents per 100,000 population has been fluctuating around 23 for the last 65 years. The peak in the late 1960s provoked a public outcry that resulted in legislation making seat belts mandatory. The smooth line is an S-curve fit.

Why the number of deaths is 23 per 100,000 per year and how society can detect a rise to, say, 28 is not clear. Rates in other countries suggest possible effects of cultural origin. For the year 1975, seven nations (Austria, Belgium, France, Denmark, Italy, Canada, and the United States) had deaths rates not far from 23.

Three countries were exceptions. For the United Kingdom, Sweden, and Japan the number was around 12. These countries had been driving on the left. If this difference is significant, exploring the phenomenon further may be interesting. Could it be that left-side drivers are less accident prone?

The number of deaths in the last 15 years suggests a downturn. Are we finally improving in car safety, or is it yet another fluctuation? American society has tolerated this level for over 60 years. A Rand analyst has put it rather bluntly: "I am sure that there is, in effect, a desirable level of automobile accidents—desirable, that is, from a broad point of view; in the sense that it is a necessary concomitant of things of greater value to society."[4]

Lacking compelling arguments to the contrary, I would offer a long-term forecast of little or no change, in what appears to be an invariant related to car safety. In fact, given that in recent years the number of deaths per 100,000 per year has been below 20—far from the "canonical" 23—I would expect a rise of about 20 percent over the next decade. Such a rise will probably be explained later as a result of the ever-increasing number of cars on the road as well as the upward drift of the speed limits from poorly tolerated low settings, already in progress.

An invariant can be thought of as a deeply rooted state of well-being that nature or society develops ways to maintain. Individuals may come forward from time to time as advocates of an apparently well-justified cause. What they do not suspect is that they are acting as unwitting agents to deeply rooted necessities for maintaining the existing balance, a balance that would have been maintained in any case. An example is Ralph Nader's crusade for car safety, *Unsafe at Any Speed*, published in the 1960s. By that time the number of fatal car accidents had already demonstrated a 40-year period of relative stability. Examining Fig. 7-2 closely, we see that the late 1960s show a peak in accidents, which must have been what prompted Nader to blow the whistle. Had he not done so, someone else would have. Alternatively, a timely social mechanism might have produced the same result: perhaps an "accidental" discovery of an effective new car safety feature.

HUMANS VERSUS MACHINES

Invariants characterize a natural equilibrium. A physiological example is that the average person sleeps during one-third of the day-night cycle. Another example is the amount of time people spend traveling daily, let us say, to work and back. Studies have shown that the optimum time is 70 minutes. People who commute for much longer resent it. Patients confined to a bed or prisoners to a small cell suffer from their confinement. It therefore seems reasonable that a balance should exist between the amount of physical and intellectual work carried out during a day. In the world of computers, software can be likened to intellect and hardware to body, and their relative importance seems to be emerging as an invariant that contradicts the best judgment of some information technology experts.

From the discovery of the wheel to the birth of the transistor, history is punctuated with milestones marking the appearance of machines that relieved humans from repetitive burdens. Industrialization featured mostly muscle-surrogate inventions, but that did not significantly decrease the number of working hours. Allowing 8 hours for sleep and a fair amount for personal matters, the time available for work cannot be far from 8 to 10 hours per day. At the same time, human nature is such that working much less than that is poorly tolerated. Cases of depression may be more frequent among people who have little to do.

Soon after the introduction of computers, the need for software gave rise to a thriving new industry, because a computer is useless until programmed to do a task. The fast growth of successful software companies triggered speculation among computer manufacturers that someday computers might be given away free; all revenue would be made from services and software. This meant that the computer industry's major effort would ultimately become the production of software.

Such a trend actually began to develop. In the 1970s, large research institutions built computer support departments heavily staffed with programmers. Some of them devoted their youth and talent to writing thousands of lines of Fortran to offer scientists the possibility of making graphs, histograms, and computer-generated drawings. But graphic capabilities were progressively transferred to the hardware. Today video terminals provide graphic capabilities without even bothering the central processing unit with such menial tasks. Meanwhile, those programmers who spent time with graphic routines moved on to higher challenges, such as increasing many-fold a computer's performance through parallel processing techniques. But these techniques were also fully incorporated into the hardware later.

A study for the years 1981 to 1988 shows that the hardware-to-software ratio of society's expenditures was stable over this time. This could be a general phenomenon implying that in Western society the natural equilibrium level wants this ratio to be about 3 to 1. The ratio reflects the homeostasis between human work (software) and machine work (hardware) in the information technology industry.

For our purposes, Fig. 7-2 is composed of two parts: a rising section closely following an S-curve and a flat one— the invariant—consisting of the ceiling of the S-curve. This interpretation gives new color to our understanding of invariants. They represent the low-growth winter season at the end of a growth process. The random fluctuations can be seen as the state of chaos encountered before and after significant steps of change, as discussed in Chap. 2. In other words, depending on the time frame, invariants can be considered as states of "temporary" equilibrium. With car accidents, a downward S-curve over the next few decades cannot be excluded. It would be the consequence of shifting trends in transportation from cars to airplanes. After all, traveling by car finds itself in the fall season of its growth process, whereas air travel finds itself in the spring season of its growth process.

DECISION NONMAKERS

Kostas Alexandrakis is the CEO of a fast-growing ready-to-assemble furniture manufacturing firm in Greece. When I asked him about his life, he said: "To be the head of a large successful business is like having mounted a lion. You simply have to go where it wants." It was obvious that his business was doing well (summer season) and that consequently his choices were limited. This is the situation whenever the rate of growth goes through big steps upward but also downward. Downward-pointing S-curves also go through seasons; in Chap. 3 we called them *negative* seasons. The rapid downward roller-coaster dip corresponds to a negative summer. Negative seasons have features in common with positive ones; for example, negative summers are times of centralization and conservatism, just as usual summers are.

Wishful strategic decisions often seem realistic in the minds of CEOs, but the results turn out negative and provoke embarrassment, if not violent opposition. This is the case when the decisions are made with no respect for the business season and the natural processes already established. The decline of coal production in the United Kingdom, one of the world's major coal producers, is an example (see Fig. 7-3)[5] The following excerpt is from my book *Predictions:*

THE DECLINE OF COAL PRODUCTION IN THE UK

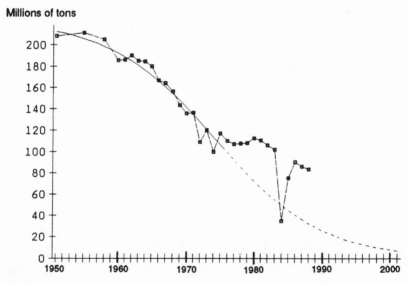

FIGURE 7-3. Annual coal production in the United Kingdom, with an S-curve fitted only to the data on the historical window 1950 to 1975. The miners' action of 1984 helped restore the natural decline halted by legislation in 1975. (The data on coal production come from the *Annual Abstract of Statistics,* a publication of the UK Government Statistics Service.)

In the substitution between primary energy sources, it is well known that the relative importance of coal has been declining in favor of oil (and to a lesser extent natural gas) since early in this century. This substitution is natural and valid in general, even if the amount of energy obtained from coal today is far from negligible. Coal's share of the total primary energy market has been decreasing worldwide for the last fifty years. Coal production in the United Kingdom started declining in 1950 and followed a usual "phasing out" course. The projection suggests that production should drop to less than 20 million tons a year by the end of the century. For the government of the United Kingdom, however, such a vision may be completely unacceptable.

In 1975 the government halted the decline in coal mining by a legislative act that fixed production at 125 million tons a year as a mechanism to absorb oil shocks. The act caused a clear deviation from the declining course of coal production, which lasted nine years. At that time miners staged the longest strike ever, bringing coal production down. The fact that the level of production dropped to what it should have been had it followed the pre-decree trajectory makes one wonder whether renewed high-production levels portend another major action by miners.

One month after the book's publication, the prediction came true. The miners did not stage a new strike, but John Major's government tried to close down 61 percent of the country's mining pits, in a move that would bring production down to just about the level of the dotted line in Fig. 7-3. The move created an uproar among mine workers, reaching the limits of a social revolution. I sent a copy of my book to Prime Minister Major, telling him that what he was trying to do was perfectly natural but that it was previous governments' decisions that made his job difficult. But things changed for the British coal industry. The 1970s were a negative summer, a season opposing change. The late 1990s are closer to the end of the declining process and therefore correspond to a negative winter, a season during which new directions and revolutionary change can be more easily implemented.

The evolution of British coal production corroborates the fact that social systems are characterized by a high resistance to change. The evolution of air transport and car populations follows smooth S-curves, showing no deviation during the two oil crises of the 1970s. Yet both means of transportation are intimately linked to the availability of oil and the general state of the economy. Social systems have an ability to compensate internally for most changes. Jay Forrester claims that up to 98 percent of all government policies may have little effect on a system's behavior.

Another source of constraint for decision makers is *optimization*. Optimization—characteristic of a summer season—reduces choice. This principle is demonstrated in closed-circuit car races such as Formula One. Without too much difficulty, a scientifically minded person can write a computer program to optimize the driver's decisions during the race. Among the data needed are the power of the car, the ratio of the gears, the total weight, the coefficient of friction between wheels and pavement, and the detailed course. Then some laws of physics must be built in: centrifugal forces, accelerations, and the like. That done, a printout can be produced that dictates the actions a driver must take to cover 50 laps of the course in the shortest possible time. After the race, the winner may be confronted with this list of actions and asked if he or she carried them out. The winner will, of course, claim that he or she was acting with free will but would have to agree that what is on the paper represents what was done; otherwise the winner would not have won.

From the moment a competitor chooses to strive for the winning place in a Formula One race, there is not much freedom left. The driver must follow the list of optimized course actions as closely as possible. Thus, the winner's actions and decisions are rather predictable, in contrast to a driver who is accident-prone or a Sunday driver who decides to stop for an unpredictable reason, such as to observe a rare bird. Decisions that can be predicted in timing, quality, and quantity are no longer decisions; they are necessities dictated by the role assumed. For a race car driver the only free choice is making mistakes. There are many ways of making mistakes, but only one way of doing it right, and that one can be forecasted.

Like race car drivers, leaders and CEOs who find their business in a summer season are constrained in their decision making. A better name for them is *optimizers*. Such a name is equally appropriate for marketers and top executives, who feel a heavy responsibility for making decisions. The gravity they see in choosing their direction causes them, at best, anxiety and, at worst, an ulcer or a heart attack. Yet they behave as optimizers whenever they enter a summer season. Their job during this time is to stay on the well-established course. To do that they need to make corrections, like drivers on a highway who are in fact continuously zigzagging in order to go straight. The best of us may make smaller and less frequent corrections, but none of us is free to make a sharp turn.

Highway driving is not particularly anxiety provoking. There is relatively little choice. There is both wisdom and comfort in the whimsical saying, "Rejoice, rejoice, we have no choice." A leader's job to a large extent is to optimize— that is, to reduce the amplitude and frequency of the corrections to be applied. The burden of such responsibility is not unbearable. If decision makers became more aware of well-established natural growth processes and of how often they do not have free choice after all, they not only would benefit from reduced stress but also would avoid a certain number of mistakes.

There is predictability associated with summer seasons. During this time the job of a successful leader should not be stressful, since there is relatively little uncertainty about the future. The future is more uncertain during a winter season, but this uncertainty is limited in time. *The future is always what it used to be.* We simply have to remember the *right* time—not the most pleasant time, which has the habit of subconsciously creeping up. The right time is four seasons ago, last "year," meaning last business cycle. The future is always the same if we put ourselves in our shoes four seasons ago. I bet there were people in the 1930s who said, "The future is no longer what it used to be."

DID MOZART DIE OF OLD AGE?

Death comes naturally in winter seasons. But it does not have to be *this* winter. You can postpone death until next winter, or even the winter after next. Cesare Marchetti was the first to associate the evolution of a person's creativity and productivity with natural growth. He assumed that a work of art or science is the final expression of a "pulse of action" that originates somewhere in the depths of the brain and works its way through many intermediate stages to produce a creation. He then studied the number of these creations over time and found that their growth followed S-shaped curves. Each curve presupposed a final ceiling, a niche size that Marchetti called a *perceived* target, since competition may prevent it from being reached. He then proceeded to study hundreds of well-documented artists and scientists. In each case, he took the total number of known creations, graphed them over time, and determined the S-shaped curve that would best connect these data points. He found that most people died close to having realized their perceived potential. In his words:

> To illustrate further what I mean...consider the amount of beans a man has in his bag and the amount left when he finally dies. Looking at the cases mentioned here...I find that the leftover beans are usually five to ten percent of the total. Apparently when Mozart died at 35 years of age, he had already said what he had to say.[6]

The idea is intriguing. Obviously people's productivity increases and decreases with time. Youngsters cannot produce much because they have to learn first. Old people may become exhausted of ideas, energy, and motivation. It makes intuitive sense that productivity goes through a cycle over a person's lifetime, slowing down as it approaches the end. The cumulative productivity—the total number of works produced—could very well look like an S-shaped curve over time.

In order to check Marchetti's claims, I fit the S-shaped pattern of natural growth on Mozart's data, his musical compositions (see Fig. 7-4). I counted every composition as one unit, on the argument that a minuet at the age of 6 is no less a creative achievement than a requiem at the age of 35. The fit turned out to be successful. I found an S-curve that passed impressively close to all 31 yearly points representing the cumulative number of compositions. There were two little irregularities, however, one on each end.

The irregularity at the low end of the curve caused my computer program to include an early-missing-data parameter. The reason: better agreement between the curve and the data if 18 compositions are assumed to be missing during

MOZART (1756-1791)

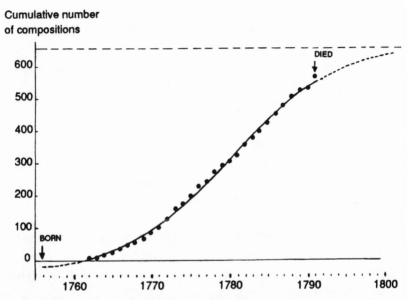

FIGURE 7-4. The best-fitting S-shaped curve implies 18 compositions "missing" between 1756 and 1762. The nominal beginning of the curve—the 1 percent level—points at Mozart's birthday. The nominal end—the 99 percent level—indicates a potential of 644 works.

Mozart's earliest years. His first recorded composition was created in 1762, when he was 6. However, the curve's nominal beginning is around 1756, Mozart's birthdate. Conclusion: Mozart was composing from the moment he was born. His first 18 compositions, however, were never recorded for "technical" reasons—the fact that he could neither write nor speak well enough to dictate them to his father.[7]

The second irregularity was at the high end of the curve, the year of Mozart's death: 1791 showed a large increase in productivity. In fact, the data point fell well above the curve, corresponding more to the productivity projected for the year 1793. What was Mozart trying to do during the last year of his life? With his creative potential determined as 644 compositions, his last composition would put him at the 91 percent level of exhaustion. Most people who die of old age have realized 90 percent of their creative potential. There was very little left for Mozart to do. His work in this world had been practically accomplished. The irregularity at the high end of his creativity curve indicated the sprint at the finish! What he had left to do was not enough to help him fight the illness that was consuming him. "Mozart died of old age" is the conclusion we would come to by looking at Fig. 7-4. Yet there is a popular belief that the world has been deprived of many musical masterpieces by his "premature" death.

In discussions with musicians, I have found that many are not shocked by the idea that Mozart may have exhausted his creative potential at the age of 35. He had already contributed so much in *every* musical form of the time that he could no longer break new ground. Of course, he could have done more of the same: more concertos, more symphonies, more trios and quartets. But all this would have represented compromised innovation. He himself wrote at the age of 21, "To live until one can no longer contribute anything new to music."[8]

His *Dissonant Quartet in C Major* K465 (1785) has been cited as evidence for Mozart's possible evolution, had he lived. I consider this an unlikely scenario. The learning curve of music lovers of that time could not accommodate the kind of music that became acceptable more than 150 years later. Mozart would have soon stopped exploring musical directions that provoked public rejection.

But Mozart did not have to die at 35 just because he had exhausted the capability to innovate in music. Cascading careers are known to exist and play a decisive role in long, happy lives. Football players do not necessarily die upon retirement from the playing ground. Many retirees embark on new activities with success. However, before contemplating rebirth or other strategic initiative toward a new lease on life, career changers need to understand and satisfy two requirements, as discussed in the following section.

A SECOND LEASE ON LIFE

From the moment I became interested in associating the S-shaped curves to people's lifetimes, I searched for failures as diligently as for successes. In that regard, I thought that an unnatural death should interrupt the evolution of a person's productivity abruptly. Consequently, I searched for famous people who died by accident, violent death, or suicide. I soon came across a new difficulty, however. What constitutes a truly unnatural death? When I tried to construct an S-curve describing Ernest Hemingway's book-writing career, his life's end turned out to look rather natural (see Fig. 7-5).

The cumulative number of books Hemingway wrote can be described well by a natural growth curve whose nominal beginning points at 1909, when he was 10 years old. The fitted curve starts in 1909 and has a ceiling of 18.[9] Since no one can reasonably expect a teenager to publish books, Hemingway's first book was not published until 14 years later. But as with other cases of pent-up demand, a blocked creative impulse gathers energy that is released during the early phases of a career. Hemingway was no exception; he produced intensely the first 3 years—"unnaturally" so, since his cumulative work grew faster than the curve. But in 1925 the publication of *In Our Time* placed him squarely on the curve, from which he did not significantly deviate until the end.

The interesting thing about Hemingway is that he

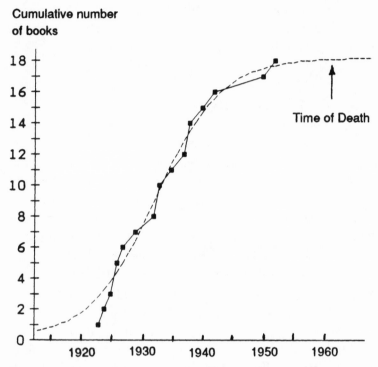

HEMINGWAY (1899-1961)

FIGURE 7-5.   The cumulative number of books published by
Hemingway.

approached smoothly the end of his book-writing career at
the age of 52. This is as Mozart did at 35, and many others
documented in my book. All died of natural causes, having
realized virtually all their creative potential. Indeed, biogra-
phers have noted that Hemingway's realization of his wan-
ing creative powers was a contributing factor in his suicide.
The S-curve depicts Hemingway's time of death as natural
even though he took his own life. But it would have been

equally natural for him to live another 20 years had he embarked on a new activity—for example, writing biographies. Alfred Hitchcock followed this course when he moved from cinema to television.

Figure 7-6 shows the number of films for which Hitchcock could claim credit at any time during his career. As a child Hitchcock manifested interest in theatrical plays,

HITCHCOCK'S TWO NICHES IN CINEMA.

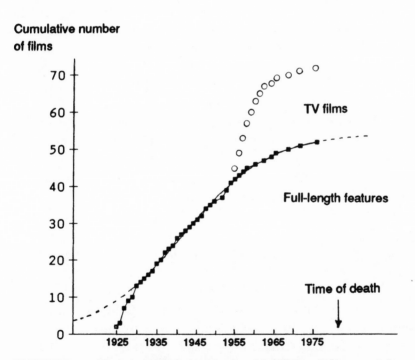

FIGURE 7-6. The squares indicate Hitchcock's full-length films, and the circles indicate the sum of both full-length and shorter television films. The fit is only to the full-length films. A smaller curve is outlined by the television films and seems to have its beginning in Hitchcock's film works.

but as a teenager he went to the cinema frequently and soon began visiting movie studios. At the age of 20 he took a modest job as a designer of titles for the silent movies of the time, pretending—something that he maintained even later—that he had no ambition to assume more responsibility. This is in contradiction to his insistence on learning everything there was to learn about filmmaking and volunteering to try his hand at any new assignment. In fact, the lower part of the curve fitted to the data of Hitchcock's full-length films seems to originate well before 1925, when his first movie appeared. This means that his impulse for direction was deeply rooted. When he finally started his career as a film director at 26, he produced prodigiously during the first 6 years, as if he were trying to "catch up"—not unlike many others discussed in *Predictions* whose early careers display a sudden release of pent-up productivity.

From 1930 onward the cumulative number of Hitchcock's full-length features grows smoothly to reach 52 by 1975. But the rate of growth is progressively lower after the mid-1950s. It is not by accident that in 1955 he was persuaded to make television films for the celebrated series *Alfred Hitchcock Presents*. The open circles on the graph represent the sum of both full-length and shorter television films. A shorter S-curve can be clearly outlined on top of the long one. This second niche contains 20 films; the process of filling it up starts in 1955 and flattens out, approaching natural completion, by 1962.

The evolution of Hitchcock's work just before he embarked on the television adventure contains a suggestive signal, a slowing-down that leads smoothly into the subsequent television activity. Statistically speaking, the small deviation of the data points around 1951 has no real significance. It coincides, however, with the period when the U.S. film industry felt most strongly the competition from the growing popularity of television. It also coincides with the time Hitchcock's main-feature career entered a period of declining growth—fall season. The television series put Hitchcock in spring again. It provided him with new potential for creativity and another high-growth period for his career. He was fortunate in his timing. New career cycles, like agricultural crops, must be seeded during the fall of the previous cycle.

There are many examples of individuals who had two and three or more cascading careers with an S-curve describing each one of them. Typically, women launch a new activity once the fertility curve ends in the early forties. Likewise, athletes and others with careers strongly dependent on physical condition often embark on more intellectual pursuits (coaching, writing, and so on). Two conditions must be satisfied for a successful career renewal. One is timing—that is, the seeds must be put down during the fall season of the previous career. The other condition is that the new activity must be sufficiently differentiated as to constitute a new "species." Mozart's timing was right. He composed the *Dissonant Quartet*—if we consider it for a moment as his attempt to branch out into a new niche for musical composition—during the fall season of his career. But the new "species" was neither differentiated enough nor gifted for survival (it was rejected as being too far ahead of its time). Mozart would have had a better chance at a second lease on life as a musicologist, a music critic, or even a writer.

MANAGING THE ENTERPRISE AFTER YEAR 2000

- We will come back to more centralized organizational models.

- A global enterprise may look like a necklace of several small or medium-size enterprises spread around the globe.

- There will be demand for MBAs, leadership training, and cross-discipline expertise.

In October 1994, the editors of *Revue Française de Gestion* (the French equivalent of the *Harvard Business Review*) celebrated their hundredth-issue anniversary by inviting world-renowned experts to answer questions on what it will be like to do business in the twenty-first century. The magazine, true to its French tradition, is more theoretical than its U.S. counterpart. Nevertheless, several Americans contributed to the issue. My contribution, reproduced below, is based entirely on natural growth processes established from studies on historical data.[1] Some of my conclusions contrasted sharply with those of the other people interviewed. For example, one prediction, which the editors chose to highlight, was a future return to more centralized organizational models. Below are my responses to all the questions, as translated from the article that was published in French in the hundredth issue of the *Revue Française de Gestion* in October 1994.

1. How will the definition itself of an enterprise evolve? What will be the consequences on the management of enterprises?

The dawn of the twenty-first century will coincide with a progressive general economic improvement. Growth rates in industry will keep increasing toward a prosperity culminating with a boom in the 2020s, not unlike the one of the 1960s. In that perspective, management policies will progressively shift from today's decentralized, segmented, and horizontal models into centralized, unified, and vertical ones. The current violent bottom-up cultural forces will weaken, permitting top-down vision-driven management styles to become commonplace again. Leadership will become more important than entrepreneurship.

But everything will not be as in the past. The irreversible consequences of persistent innovation and customization will produce an increase in the number of interactions between vendors and clients. There will be a downsizing effect on the transaction size, on many levels. Even if the economy grows only moderately, the number of transactions will increase significantly.

2. How will society evolve? What lifestyles could become decisive or problematic for the survival of enterprises in the twenty-first century?

There will be new frames of work: nomadic, teleworking, 24-hour work. The individual is not necessarily teleworking from a fixed remote location but rather, and more consistent with reality, *in movement*. Working in the premises of customers, colleagues, professional peers, and at home, the information worker becomes location-independent and, by doing so, changes forever the parameters of enterprise computing.

3. In what domains will managers and enterprises have to learn the most? Modify their old ways?

The capacity to learn and adapt will play a progressively crucial role for the individual as well as for the enterprise. By the end of the first decade in the next millennium, the growing need for leadership will give rise to a wave of leadership-training institutions (the comeback of MBAs, business schools in general, and, more important, leadership schools). Management teams will have to learn to adapt rapidly to cultural changes. For example, a general manager should be able to pass from a "macho" management style to a more "feminine" style and even to a style of "neutral" gender in an efficient and fluid way. Another major adaptation will be to learn how to deal with the many-fold increase in the number of small transactions and relationships arising from the general downsizing effect mentioned in the answer to question 1.

4. What particular developments will influence the relationships between managers of different functions and their environments: personnel, clients, suppliers, distributors, stockholders, and so on?

Salaries will be decoupled from power. We could imagine that a knowledgeable consultant, or a Nobel prize researcher, earns more than the general manager of his or her enterprise. More and more enterprises will ensure employability (skills and training) rather than employment (fixed jobs). A continuous training and updating of employee skills will make employees less vulnerable to restructuring and bankruptcies and will create mobility and flexibility in the human resource market. Intermediation will weaken, as a result of technology and the desire to increase profits.

Manufacturing will become agile rather than lean, also demanding flexibility. Components, modularity, and custom-tailored orders (at times through three-dimensional information systems) will become available as a response to increasing demand. Markets will become collections of microniches, as usually happens during the early stages of a new industry's growth.

5. Can you imagine significant particular developments in the future relationship between state and commerce (regulations, industrial policies, subsidies, and the like)?

As faster and faster means of transportation become available (the hypersonic plane will link the whole world into one community by permitting people to go from one point on the earth to another within the 70-minute daily quota of personal travel time), businesspeople will be able to work anywhere without abandoning their home nest. Globalization in this sense will not affect national identity. Cultural diversity will be preserved, and state and enterprise will become "transparent" to each other.

However, at the level of the individual, social security and human rights—established priorities in the West—will rapidly become standard in the central and eastern European countries (for example, as a chapter in such certification standards as the ISO 9000, established in the European Economic Community).

6. What will the consequences be to the enterprise of globalization and the increasing migration of manufacturing and markets?

The need to do business globally and continuously (24 hours a day) will dictate an increase in partnerships and relationships between enterprises in different geographical locations. A global small or medium-size enterprise (SME) may look like a necklace of several SMEs spread around the globe but be informationally linked.

One problem will be the excessively high salaries of Western professionals. Manufacturing and commerce in general will keep migrating toward developing countries. Consequently, the third world will come closer to the West, thus increasing the gap between third and fourth worlds (underdeveloped countries of Africa and Asia) and provoking worldwide tensions.

7. Has on-line management in its present form (flexibility, office automation, and so on) achieved all it can? What else can we still expect from information technology?

The main benefits from information technology have not yet been seen. They consist of making it possible for the professional to move and communicate wirelessly while working efficiently. An "animated" network will become the system. The computer will be reduced to a simple component that serves as the "glue" for all operations. Other components will offer access to multimedia knowledge banks. Despite today's trends indicating a progressively important role for software and services compared with hardware, an equilibrium (homeostasis) will eventually be reached between "soft" and "hard," between service and product revenues.

8. How do you see the evolution of the time allocation of managers and other members of the enterprise?

Long-range strategic planning will come back into fashion early in the next century. Tolerance for new styles of work will increase. Empowerment will slowly lose popularity, and a more centralized control will eventually lead once more to strong leadership, stovepipes, and conservatism (around 2020).

9. Which domains or disciplines of management (such as marketing) will become more important? Which will become less important?

As the economy picks up, less importance will be attributed to an opportunistic workforce and more to strong leadership. The evolution of human resources (workforce skill) in general will follow suit. Today's entrepreneurs and generalists will be less in demand, and specialists will be recruited for the intensive product innovation (R&D work) and the building up of agile and efficient manufacturing capabilities.

10. In your field, what would you like to work on? On what should researchers—if you are not one yourself—generally concentrate during the next 20 years?

Cross-disciplinary endeavors carry a large potential for growth and success. By contrast, traditional disciplines are saturating, having reached their zenith of success.

Future leaders are likely to seek out the opinions of philosophers and artists in addition to those of traditional scientists. Cross-disciplinary specialists are emerging as a promising new species for management research.

EPILOGUE

- *S-curves* and *life cycles* reveal how growth potential becomes realized over time. They are endowed with predictive powers, because they show the most economic paths. They can help you plan your actions *just in time*.
- The *four-seasons metaphor* guides decision making throughout the life cycle. Success and failure, order and chaos, predictability, leadership, creativity, and excellence, all depict some kind of "seasonality." Identifying your season is key to a winning strategy.
- *Systematic techniques* and *tools* can help you determine with precision the S-curve, the life cycle, the season you are in, its duration, your actual position in it, and the best-fit strategy.

The most respected laws of physics are the simple ones. The simpler the law, the more fundamental it is, and the broader its domain of application. This is the case with natural growth in competition, the law that follows the S-shaped pattern. The pattern has an associated life cycle—namely, a beginning, a growth phase, a maturity phase, a declining phase, and an end. Moreover, these phases match the seasons metaphor in many respects, with the end corresponding to a second winter.

Consequently, S-curves, life cycles, and seasonal patterns can be used to obtain insights not only for species and products but for *any* situation where competition and growth play an important role. Technologies, markets, business units, companies, and whole industries come and go along S-curves, are characterized by a life cycle, and experience seasonal variations. The first thing to do before setting any strategy is to identify your position on the curves and in the season. You can then embark on paths of least resistance and make decisions in accordance with the "spirit of the times."

Fundamental laws are not forgiving. It is unwise to try to fight a well-established natural growth process. It is far more efficient to anticipate, prepare, and tune in with what is happening by using least-resistance paths. A company's turnaround is effectively tantamount to the death of the old company in favor of the birth of a new one. This is a necessary condition, creating a possibility but not a guarantee for new growth. By contrast, a long life cycle can be secured by identifying and supporting the company's various units individually and in accordance with the season of each. For example, invest in units in spring season and replace units in fall season.

Winter is the season when changes are easiest to implement. Yet even in winter the biggest resistance to change should be expected from the human element, the company's culture. Culture is the collective programming of the mind that distinguishes human communities into "species." It is responsible for wars. People are the only animals that destroy "their own" through war, an act that is basically an expression of intercultural competition. Cultural forces influence the rate of most social change. Culture represents the inertia (mass) that resists the implementation of leaders' visions. Rich cultures, often stemming from long traditions, tend to be noninnovating. Cultural changes are so slow that long-term thinking is essential, and perseverance is more important than argument.

One way to deal with resistive cultural forces is to involve people in the decision-making process. This approach works well with small groups such as executive teams and management boards. Our experience at Growth Dynamics has been that on-line interactive tools aid decision making in three ways:

- They extract conscious and subconscious knowledge from informed and experienced executives. Combining intelligent people with intelligent tools produces results that neither could produce separately.
- They ensure the participants' buy-in, involving them in the conclusion-arriving process.
- They achieve quick results. Looking at the big picture helps participants arrive at difficult decisions within a short time.

The metaphor of seasons in business combines diversity with predictability. Things will keep changing, but in some ways the change can be predicted. Springs will always follow winters, and summers will lead into falls. But all springs will have common elements and so will all falls. Contrary to popular belief, the most desirable climate is not found on tropical islands like Mauritius and the Seychelles. It is a temperate climate with large and regular seasonal variation. That has been the cradle of most great civilizations. History is poor in significant cultures that emerged from the arctic or the tropics, the former perhaps because of conditions hostile to life and the latter mostly because of lack of variation and motivation. Despite an idyllic setting, tropical islands are rather sterile.

The expulsion of Adam and Eve from Paradise may have been, after all, the original blessing.

S-CURVES: MATHEMATICAL FORMULATIONS

The behavior of populations growing under Darwinian competition has been the object of much discussion in the scientific literature.[1] Below is a simplified formulation for the cases considered in this book.

ONE SPECIES ONLY

An example of the case of one species is a population of bacteria growing in a bowl of broth. The bacteria act as the agent that transforms the chemicals present in the broth into bacteria. The rate of this transformation is proportional to the number of bacteria present and the concentration of transformable chemicals.

All transformable chemicals will eventually become bacteria. Broth chemicals can therefore be measured in terms of bacterial bodies. If we call $N(t)$ the number of bacteria at time t, and M the amount of transformable chemicals at time 0 (before multiplication starts), the Verhulst equation (the mathematical formulation of the law that gives rise to an S-curve) can be written as

$$\frac{dN}{dt} = aN \frac{M - N}{M} \tag{1}$$

and its solution is

$$N(t) = \frac{M}{1 + e^{-(at+b)}} \tag{2}$$

with b a constant locating the process in time.

We can manipulate mathematically Eq. 2 in order to put it in the form

$$\frac{N(t)}{M - N(t)} = e^{(at+b)} \tag{3}$$

Taking the logarithm of both sides, we obtain a relationship linear with time, thus transforming the S-shaped curve of Eq. 2 into the straight line of the equation $at + b$. The numerator of the left side of Eq. 3 is the new population, and the denominator indicates the space still remaining empty in the niche. In the case of one-to-one substitutions, the numerator is the size of the *new*, and the denominator is the size of the *old* at any given time. If on the vertical logarithmic scale we indicate the fractional market share instead of the ratio *new/old*, we obtain the so-called logistic scale, in which 100 percent goes to plus infinity and 0 percent to minus infinity.

M is often referred to as the niche capacity, the ceiling of the population $N(t)$ at the end of growth. In order for Eq. 1 to be solved, M must be constant throughout the growth process, but this requirement can be relaxed for one-to-one substitutions.

MANY COMPETITORS IN A NICHE

Even though the case of many species in the same niche has been studied in detail, for practical reasons in industrial applications we consider only two competitors. All many-competitor situations can be reduced to a two-competitor picture by considering the competitor of interest and grouping all the others together. This formalism is ideal when there are indeed two main competitors in the market, as with mobile phones in the United States. It is also a good approximation when the market leader happens to lead all others by a large margin. The case of many small players may require further segmentation of the market into microniches.

Equation 1 can be rewritten for two competitors X and Y as follows:

$$\frac{dX}{dt} = a_x X - b_x X^2 \tag{4}$$

$$\frac{dY}{dt} = a_y Y - b_y Y^2 \tag{5}$$

An interaction between the two competitors can be expressed in general terms via two coupling constants c_{xy} and c_{yx}, which are used to transform Eqs. 4 and 5 into a system of coupled differential equations:

$$\frac{dX}{dt} = a_x X - b_x X^2 + c_{xy} XY$$

$$\frac{dY}{dt} = a_y Y - b_y Y^2 + c_{yx} YX$$

This system of equations contains all fundamental parameters that determine the rate of growth—namely, the power of each "species" to multiply (a is related to attractiveness), the limitation of the niche capacity (b is related to niche size), and the interaction with the other "species" (c is the coupling). The signs of c_{xy} and c_{yx} determine the type of competition according to the definitions of Chap. 6.

This system of equations is nonlinear and cannot be solved analytically. However, solutions can be found numerically. Pielou has recast this system of differential equations into a system of difference equations.[2] The new system can now be solved via numerical iterative techniques.

To use Pielou's formulation, we need to introduce a number of new constants: λ_x, β_x, λ_y, and β_y, as defined below. Under the assumption that X is the incumbent and Y the attacker, the attacker's advantage A, and the defender's counterattack D, discussed in Chap. 6, can be expressed in terms of the coupling constants c_{xy} and c_{yx}, respectively, as follows:

$$X(t + 1) = \frac{\lambda_x X(t)}{1 + \beta_x X(t) - A\,\beta_x\,Y(t)}$$

$$Y(t + 1) = \frac{\lambda_y Y(t)}{1 + \beta_y Y(t) - D\,\beta_y\,X(t)}$$

where $\lambda = e^a$ and $\beta = \dfrac{b(e^a - 1)}{a}$ for X and Y and

$$A = \frac{c_{xy}}{\beta_x} \quad \text{and} \quad D = \frac{c_{yx}}{\beta_y}$$

These formulations are used in the software tools developed by Growth Dynamics.

Carl Pistorius and James Utterback have explored phase diagrams, $X(t)$ versus $Y(t)$, in which directional derivatives can indicate preferred directions for action.[3] This subject needs further study and development toward practical applications.

ECONOMIES OF SCALE AND PRICE ELASTICITY

Price elasticity relates the volume of sales to the price. Obviously, the lower the price, the higher the number of transactions. Therefore volume must be inversely proportional to price. In order not to lose any generality, we assume:

$$V = \frac{C}{P^n} \qquad (1)$$

where C is a constant, V is the volume of sales in dollars, and P is the price.

We can now deduce that for two different prices, the volumes change as follows:

$$\frac{V_2}{V_1} = \left(\frac{P_1}{P_2}\right)^n \qquad (2)$$

which, for small changes, can be mathematically approximated as

$$\frac{\Delta V}{V} = -n \, \frac{\Delta P}{P} \tag{3}$$

Equation 3 defines n as price elasticity, relating a change in volume ΔV to a change in price ΔP.

In Chap. 4 we determined the computer price elasticity $n = 1.09$ by fitting Eq. 1 to the revenue distribution from computer sales in the range \$10,000 to \$10 million. This is a quantitative determination of price elasticity. Volume changes can then be rigorously related to price changes. For example, a 10 percent drop (rise) in price will increase (decrease) the revenue by 10.9 percent.

WHY THE INDUSTRIAL REVOLUTION SUCCEEDED

Manufacturing costs grow like an *area* variable but the utility produced grows like a *volume* variable. To understand this, think of manufacturing a container. Costs will be proportional to the total surface, but the container's usefulness—what customers pay money for—is the volume it encloses. Consequently, costs and volumes are related as follows:

$$\frac{V_2}{V_1} = \left(\frac{C_1}{C_2}\right)^{3/2} \tag{4}$$

The exponent 3/2 agrees well with the value 1.6 experimentally established, and quoted in chemical engineering handbooks for process industries.

The success of the industrial revolution becomes demystified if we compare Eq. 2 with Eq. 4. If all prices were cut in half, the money available would cover twice the volume of transactions. But doubling the volume would incur only 26 percent more manufacturing costs (from Eq. 4)—hence the profit!

Obviously reality is not that simple, and elasticity can be substantially different from unit. But Eq. 4 implies more important rewards for bigger volumes. The moral of the story is along the lines of "bigness is goodness"—that is, the greater the volume, the greater the profit. This is not the entire story, however.

We saw in Chap. 5 that the S-shaped learning process is intimately related to economies of scale. The reasoning was different there. We did not argue in terms of surface and volume variables or in terms of available money and how many transactions it can support. We simply invoked the similarity between the experimental industry curve and the inverse of the S-curve expression. The moral of that comparison was that learning alone could have accounted for the reduction of costs with volume.

The truth probably involves both phenomena, voluminous production and learning. But I am convinced that learning will play a progressively important role. In the manufacturing of microprocessors, for example, the surface-to-volume argument breaks down. The argument will break down further with services, telecommunications, and the Internet.

NOTES
AND SOURCES

PROLOGUE

1. Joseph F. Coates, "What to Do When You Don't Know What You Are Doing," *Technological Forecasting and Social Change,* vol. 50, 1995, pp. 249–252.
2. See Jay W. Forrester, "System Dynamics and the Lessons of 35 Years," in Kenyon B. De Greene, ed., *A Systems-Based Approach to Policy Making,* Kluwer Academic, The Netherlands, 1991.
3. Charles Handy, *The Empty Raincoat,* Hutchinson, London, 1994.
4. In several annual international symposia on forecasting that I have attended, there has always been a session devoted to this question. The same was true with the conference on "Diffusion of Technologies and Social Behavior," August 1989, Laxenburg, Austria.
5. Forrester, "System Dynamics."

CHAPTER ONE

1. Cesare Marchetti is a physicist at the International Institute for Applied Systems Analysis in Laxenburg, Austria. He uses laws from biology and physics to describe social phenomena. He is the person who indoctrinated me into S-curves and changed the course of my life.
2. *The S-Shaped Adventure* was the original title of my first book. The title was changed by the publisher into *Predictions: Society's Telltale*

Signature Reveals the Past and Forecasts the Future, Simon & Schuster, New York, 1992.

3. The graph was published in my book *Predictions.*

4. This graph has been adapted from one published in Cesare Marchetti, "The Automobile in a System Context: The Past 80 Years and the Next 20 Years," *Technological Forecasting and Social Change,* vol. 23, 1983, pp. 3–23.

5. J. C. Fisher and R. H. Pry, "A Simple Substitution Model of Technological Change," *Technological Forecasting and Social Change,* vol. 3, 1971, pp. 75–88.

6. Alfred J. Lotka, *Elements of Physical Biology,* Williams & Wilkins Co., Baltimore, 1925.

7. Richard Foster, *Innovation: The Attacker's Advantage,* Macmillan, London, 1986.

8. Charles Handy, *The Age of Paradox,* Harvard Business School Press, Boston, 1994.

9. Hen Blanchard and Terry Waghorn, *Mission Possible,* McGraw-Hill, New York, 1996.

10. This graph has been constructed from data digitized from a graph in N. Nakicenovic, "The Automobile Road to Technological Change," *Technological Forecasting and Social Change,* vol. 29, 1986, pp. 309–340.

11. Adrian Slywotzky, *Value Migration,* Harvard Business School Press, Boston, 1996.

12. This graph was constructed from data digitized from graphs in *Value Migration,* ibid.

13. Modis, *Predictions.*

14. The chaotic fluctuations are discussed in Chap. 3, but for an in-depth study see Theodore Modis, "Fractal Aspects of Natural Growth," *Technological Forecasting and Social Change,* vol. 47, 1994, pp. 63–73.

15. The graph can be found in Modis, *Predictions,* Fig. 10.3.

CHAPTER TWO

1. Alfred J. Lotka, *Elements of Physical Biology,* Williams & Wilkins Co., Baltimore, 1925.

2. Nikolai D. Kondratieff, "The Long Wave in Economic Life," *Review of Economic Statistics*, vol. 17, 1935, pp. 105–115. Also, Nikolai D. Kondratieff, *Les Grands Cycles de la Conjoncture*, Economica, Paris, 1992.

3. The chaotic fluctuations are discussed in Chap. 3, but for an in-depth study see Theodore Modis, "Fractal Aspects of Natural Growth," *Technological Forecasting and Social Change*, vol. 47, 1994, pp. 63–73.

4. W. Brian Arthur, "Positive Feedbacks in the Economy," *Scientific American*, February 1990, pp. 80–85.

5. As reported by David Clutterbuck and Stuart Crainer in *Makers of Management*, MacMillan, London, 1990.

6. This is one of several interactive user-friendly software tools developed at Growth Dynamics.

7. See T. Modis, *Predictions*, Simon & Schuster, New York, 1992, Chap. 5.

8. See Adrian J. Slywotzky, *Value Migration*, Harvard Business School Press, Boston, 1996.

CHAPTER THREE

1. See Theodore Modis and Alain Debecker, "Chaoslike States Can Be Expected before and after Logistic Growth," *Technological Forecasting and Social Change*, vol. 41, 1992, pp. 111–120.

2. This figure reproduces in part a drawing from J. Ausubel, A. Grubler, and N. Nakicenovic, "Carbon Dioxide Emission in a Methane Economy," *Climatic Change*, vol. 12, 1988, p. 254.

3. The former has been suggested by Cesare Marchetti. The latter is a result of private communications with physicist Simon van der Meer and, independently, Professor Michael Royston of Geneva's International Management Institute.

4. Gerhard Mensch, *Stalemate in Technology: Innovations Overcome the Depression*, Ballinger, Cambridge, Mass., 1979.

5. We saw in Chap. 2 a qualitative way, and in Chap. 5 we examine a quantitative way.

6. See, for example, *The Power of Strategic Evolution* and *Second Lease on Life* from Growth Dynamics.

CHAPTER FOUR

1. This definition was first given by Cesare Marchetti. See "Branching Out into the Universe," in Nehojsa Nakicenovic and Amulf Grubler (eds.), *Diffusion of Technologies and Social Behavior*, Springer-Verlag, Laxenburg, Austria, 1991.

2. See Cesare Marchetti, "On 1012: A Check on Earth Carrying Capacity for Man," in Report RR-78-7, May 1978, International Institute of Advanced Systems Analysis, Laxenburg, Austria; and in *Energy*, vol. 4, 1979, pp. 1107–1117.

3. As quoted by Kevin Kelly in *Out of Control*, Addison-Wesley, Reading, Mass., 1994.

4. Ibid.

5. James Lovelock, *The Ages of Gaia*, Oxford University Press, Oxford, UK, 1989.

6. Kelly, *Out of Control*, pp. 362–363.

7. Ibid.

8. See Stanley Davis and Bill Davidson, *Vision 2020*, Simon & Schuster, New York, 1991.

9. Theodore Modis, "Fractal Aspects of Natural Growth," *Technological Forecasting and Social Change*, vol. 47, 1994, pp. 63–73.

10. See Theodore Modis, *Predictions*, Simon & Schuster, New York, 1992, pp. 178–179.

11. See Modis, "Fractal Aspects."

CHAPTER FIVE

1. D. Robert Buzzell and T. Beadley Gale, *The PIMS Principles: Linking Strategy to Performance*, The Free Press, New York, 1987.

2. Growth Dynamics is the name of the company I founded in Geneva, Switzerland, in 1994. The tool in question is called *The Power of Strategic Evolution*.

3. See Theodore Modis, "Learning from Experience in Positioning New Computer Products," *Technological Forecasting and Social Change*, vol. 41, 1992, pp. 391–399.

4. See Theodore Modis, *Predictions,* Simon & Schuster, New York, 1992, pp. 97–105.
5. T. Modis and A. Debecker, "Determining the Service Life Cycle of Computers," in N. Nakicenovic and A. Grubler, eds., *Diffusion of Technologies and Social Behavior,* Springer-Verlag, Laxenburg, Austria, 1991.
6. G. W. Potts, "Exploit Your Product's Service Life Cycle," *Harvard Business Review,* vol. 66, 1988, pp. 32–36.

CHAPTER SIX

1. These definitions and subsequent discussion originate in C. Farrell, "Survival of the Fittest Technologies," *New Scientist,* vol. 137, 1993, p. 35.
2. Kristina Smitalova and Stefan Sujan, *A Mathematical Treatment of Dynamical Models in Biological Science,* Ellis Horwood, West Sussex, UK, 1991. Actually, credit for the original classification must be given to E. Odum (1971) and M. Williamson (1972). (See Bibliography.)
3. The data come from C. Farrell, "A Theory of Technological Progress," *Technological Forecasting and Social Change,* vol. 44, 1993, p. 161. Missing data points have been interpolated.
4. Frank Sulloway, *Born to Rebel,* Pantheon, Harvard University Press, Boston, 1996.
5. The truly independent variables are *attractiveness, time constant,* and *occupancy,* the last two defined below. They are related to but different from the parameters accessible to change. Consequently, some parameters will change together.

The *time constant* of the multiplication process is defined as: *time constant* = 1/log *(attractiveness)*.

The *occupancy* is defined as: *occupancy* = 1/[*(time constant)* × *(niche size)*].

See Appendix A for technical details on how the parameters are related between them.

6. This description has been taken from Farrell, "Theory of Technological Progress."

7. The data come from Farrell, "Theory of Technological Progress." Missing data points have been interpolated.

CHAPTER SEVEN

1. The graphs have been adapted from Cesare Marchetti, "Energy Systems—The Broader Context," *Technological Forecasting and Social Change*, vol. 14, 1979, pp. 191–203.

2. The title and the central idea of this section come from John D. Williams, "The Nonsense about Safe Driving," *Fortune*, vol. 58, 1958, pp. 118–119.

3. A similar graph and many of these arguments were first reported in 1982 by Cesare Marchetti, "The Automobile in a System Context: The Past 80 Years and the Next 20 Years," *Technological Forecasting and Social Change*, vol. 23, 1983, pp. 3–23. The data in Fig. 7-2 come from the *Statistical Abstracts of the United States*, U.S. Department of Commerce, Bureau of the Census; also from the *Historical Statistics of the United States, Colonial Times to 1970*, vols. 1 and 2, Bureau of the Census, Washington, D.C., 1976.

4. Williams, "Nonsense about Safe Driving."

5. A different graph with partial data was originally used by Cesare Marchetti to illustrate these ideas in the article entitled "Energy Systems—the Broader Context."

6. See Cesare Marchetti, *Action Curves and Clockwork Geniuses*, International Institute of Advanced System Analysis, Laxenburg, Austria, April 1985.

7. See T. Modis, *Predictions*, Chap. 4.

8. Jean and Brigitte Massin, *Wolfgang Amadeus Mozart*, Fayard, Paris, 1978.

9. The data come from Philip Young and Charles W. Mann, *The Hemingway Manuscripts: An Inventory*, Pennsylvania State University Press, University Park, Pa., 1969. Also from Audrey Hanneman, *Ernest Hemingway: A Comprehensive Biography*, Princeton University Press, Princeton, N.J., 1967.

CHAPTER EIGHT

1. "L'avenir de la gestion vu par Théodore Modis: 'On reviendra aux modèles d'organisation centralisés,'" *Revue Française de Gestion,* no. 100, October 1994.

APPENDIX A

1. E. W. Montroll and N. S. Goel, "On the Volterra and Other Nonlinear Models of Interacting Populations," *Review of Modern Physics,* vol. 43, 1971, p. 231; M. Peschel and W. Mendel, *Leben wir in einer Volterra Welt?* Akademie Verlag, Berlin, 1983; P. F. Verhulst, "Recherches Mathématiques sur la loi d'Accroissement de la Population," *Nouveaux Memoires de l'Académie Royale des Sciences et des Belles-Lettres de Bruxelles,* vol. 18, 1845, pp. 1–40; J. B. S. Haldane, "The Mathematical Theory of Natural and Artificial Selection," *Transactions, Cambridge Philosophical Society,* vol. 23, 1924, pp. 19–41; Alfred J. Lotka, *Elements of Physical Biology,* Williams & Wilkins, Baltimore, 1925.

2. E. C. Pielou, *An Introduction to Mathematical Ecology,* Wiley Interscience, New York, 1969.

3. C. W. Pistorius and J. M. Utterback, "The Death Knells of Mature Technologies," *Technological Forecasting and Social Change,* vol. 50, 1995, pp. 133–151.

BIBLIOGRAPHY

Arrow, J. Kenneth, and David Pines. 1988. *The Economy as an Evolving Complex System,* Philip W. Anderson, ed.. New York: Addison-Wesley.

Arthur, W. 1987. *The Niche in Competition and Evolution.* New York: Wiley.

Basalla, G. 1988. *The Evolution of Technology.* Cambridge: Cambridge University Press.

Cooper, R. G., and E. J. Kleinschmidt. 1990. *New Products: The Key Factors in Success.* Chicago: American Marketing Association.

Davis, Stanley, and Bill Davidson. 1991. *2020 Vision.* New York: Simon & Schuster.

Dawkins, Richard. 1976. *The Selfish Gene.* Oxford University Press.

Dennett, Daniel C. 1995. *Darwin's Dangerous Idea: Evolution and the Meanings of Life.* New York: Simon & Schuster.

Drucker, P. F. 1985. The Discipline of Innovation. *Harvard Business Review.* May–June, p. 67.

_____. 1992. *Post-Capitalist Society.* New York: The Free Press.

Farrell, C. 1993. Survival of the Fittest Technologies. *New Scientist* vol. 137, p. 35.

_____. 1993. A Theory of Technological Progress. *Technological Forecasting and Social Change,* vol. 44, p. 161.

Fisher, J. C., and R. H. Pry. 1971. A Simple Substitution Model of Technological Change. *Technological Forecasting and Social Change,* vol. 3, pp. 75–88.

Forrester, Jay. 1977. Growth Cycles. *De Economist,* vol. 125, pp. 525–543.

_____. 1991. System Dynamics and the Lessons of 35 Years, in *A Systems-Based Approach to Policy Making*. Kenyon B. De Green (ed.). The Netherlands: Kluwer Academic.

Foster, Richard. 1986. *Innovation: The Attacker's Advantage*. London: Macmillan.

Fourier, François. 1972. The Economics of Harmony. *Selections from the Works of Fourier*. Julia Franklin (trans.). New York: Gordon Press.

Gause, G. F. 1932. Experimental Studies on the Struggle for Existence. *Journal of Experimental Biology*, vol. 9, p. 389.

Gleick, James. 1987. *Chaos*. New York: Viking.

Handy, Charles. 1994. *The Empty Raincoat*. London: Hutchinson.

Hofbauer, J., and K. Sigmund. 1988. *The Theory of Evolution and Dynamical Systems*. Cambridge: Cambridge University Press.

Kelly, Kevin. 1994. *Out of Control: The New Biology of Machines, Social Systems, and the Economic World*. New York: Addison Wesley.

Kingsland, Sharon E. 1985. *Modeling Nature*. Chicago University Press.

Krebs, C. J. 1985. *Ecology*. New York: Harper & Row.

Land, George, and Beth Jarman. 1992. *Break-Point and Beyond*. New York: Harper Business.

Linstone, Harold, and Ian Mitroff. 1994. *The Challenge of the 21st Century: Managing Technology and Ourselves in a Shrinking World*. Albany, N.Y.: State University of New York Press.

Lotka, A. J. 1925. *Elements of Physical Biology*. Baltimore: Williams & Wilkins.

Lovelock, James. 1989. *The Ages of Gaia*. Oxford: Oxford University Press.

Marchetti, Cesare. 1986. Infrastructures for Movement. *Technological Forecasting and Social Change*, vol. 32, p. 373.

Margulis, Lynn, and Rene Fester (eds.). 1991. *Symbiosis as a Source of Evolutionary Innovation: Speciation and Morphogenesis*. Cambridge, Mass.: MIT Press.

Miller, Lawrence M. 1989. *Barbarians to Bureaucrats*. New York: C. N. Potter.

Mensch, Gerhard. 1979. *Stalemate in Technology: Innovations Overcome the Depression*. Cambridge, Mass.: Ballinger.

Modis, T. 1992. *Predictions: Society's Telltale Signature Reveals the Past and Forecasts the Future*. New York: Simon & Schuster.

_____. 1996. Taking Strategy Cues from Mother Nature. *Handbook of Business Strategy.* New York: Faulkner & Gray, p. 59.

Morrison, I. 1996. *The Second Curve.* London: Nicholas Brealey Publishing.

Nakicenovic, N., and A. Grubler (eds.). 1991. *Diffusion of Technologies and Social Behavior.* Laxenburg, Austria: Springer-Verlag.

Odum, E. 1971. *Fundamentals of Ecology.* London: Saunders.

Pianca, E. R. 1983. *Evolutionary Ecology.* New York: Harper & Row.

Pielou, E. C. 1969. *An Introduction to Mathematical Ecology.* New York: Wiley Interscience.

Pistorius, C. W. I., and J. M. Utterback. 1995. The Death Knells of Mature Technologies. *Technological Forecasting and Social Change,* vol. 50, p. 215.

_____, and J. M. Utterback. 1997. Multi-Mode Interaction among Technologies. *Research Policy,* vol. 26, pp. 67–84.

Porter, M. E. 1980. *Competitive Strategy.* New York: The Free Press.

_____, Roper, A. T., T. W. Mason, et al. 1991. *Forecasting and Management of Technology.* New York: Wiley.

Rothschild, M. 1990. *Bionomics.* New York: Henry Holt.

Schnaars, S. P. 1994. *Managing Imitation Strategies.* New York: The Free Press.

Schumpeter, Joseph A. 1939. *Business Cycles.* New York: McGraw-Hill.

Slywotzky, Adrian J. 1996. *Value Migration: How to Think Several Moves Ahead of the Competition.* Boston: Harvard Business School Press.

Smitalova, Kristina, and Stefan Sujan. 1991. *A Mathematical Treatment of Dynamical Models in Biological Science.* West Sussex, U.K.: Ellis Horwood.

Sterman, John D. 1986. The Economic Long Wave: Theory and Evidence. *System Dynamics Review,* vol. 2, pp. 87–125.

Twiss, Brian. 1974. *Managing Technology Innovation.* New York: Longman.

Utterback, J. M. 1994. *Mastering the Dynamics of Innovation.* Boston: Harvard Business School Press.

Van Der Erve, Marc. 1994. *Evolution Management.* Oxford: Butterworth-Heinemann.

Vogel, Steve. 1994. *Life in Moving Fluids: The Physical Biology of Flow.* Princeton, N.J.: Princeton University Press.

Volterra, V. 1931. *Leçons sur la théorie mathématique de la lutte pour la vie*. Paris: Gauthier-Villars.

Waldrop, M. Mitchell. 1992. *Complexity: The Emerging Science at the Edge of Order and Chaos*. New York: Simon & Schuster.

Williamson, M. 1972. *The Analysis of Biological Populations*. London: Edward Arnold.

INDEX

Page numbers in **bold** refer to principal discussions.
Page numbers in *italics* refer to figures.

acceleration, 48
accessories, 123
accidents, 136, **139–142**, 144
   motor-vehicle, *140*
accounting, 20, *21*, 45
acrobats, 108
administrator, 41, 54
adolescence, 31
advertising, 37, 69, **117**,
   127–129, **131–132**
Africa, 163
aging, *44*
AIDS, 53
Airbus, 95
Aladdin's lantern, 2
Alpha, 60, 94
amensalism, 123, *125*
Apple, 33, 107–108
aristocrats, 53–54
art, 45, 61, 106, 149
Arthur Andersen, 20, *21*, 22, 28,
   73
Asia, 79, 163
attacker's advantage, 119–120,
   122, 125–126, 129
attractiveness, 118, 127, *128*,
   129, 132, 171, 181

baby, 97, 98

back to basics, 39
ballpoint, 64, 123–126, *125*
Barbarians to Bureaucrats, 54,
   186
Bayer, 64
BCG matrix, 4, 43–46
Bell Labs, 54
benchmarking, 33, 38–39
Berlin, 66, 67, 183
Beta, 33
Bethlehem Steel, 55
billiard balls, 136
biochemistry, 79
biologists, 18, 83, 119
Blanchard, 3, 19, 178
Boeing, 95
Bogomolov, 65
bonds, 40, 52
books, 3, 153, *154*
Boston Consulting Group, 4, 24,
   43
BPR, 33, 35
branding, *44*
builder, 54
bureaucracy, 29
bureaucrats, 31, 33–34, 37, 39,
   41
Burroughs, 72
business cycle, **29–30**, 32, 50,
   90, 149

business unit, 29, 64, 75, 78, 165
business units, 35

cannibalization, 16
career, 9, 50, 63, 153–155, 157
carpets, 128–129, *130*, 132
cars, 16–17, 19, *20*, 22, 23, 101,
    117, 123, 139–141, 144
cash cows, 38, 43
catching-up effect, 59, 60
CDI, 3
cellular phones, 28
centralization, 67–70, 73, 76, 145
CEOs, 7, 55, 104, 145, 148
chaos, 33–34, 36, 38, *42*, **57**,
    58, **60–61**, *62*, 65, 68, 71,
    83, 86–89, 102, 144,
    165
character displacement, 126
chess, 87
children, 97, 127
cinema, 122, 155, 156
client, 75, 77, 100
clients, 75, 76, 160, 161
coal, 4, 26–27, 138, 145–147,
    182
Coates, 1, 177
coevolution, 83, 86
comedy, 41
commensalism, 123–124
commodities, 40, 52
commodity-like, 99
Commodore, 28
communism, 65–66
competition, 4, 6, 10–11, 14, 16,
    18–19, 31, 34, 44, 50, 52,
    78, 83, 84, 86, 88, 103,
    108–109, 114, **117**,
    120–124, **126–127**, *128*,

competition (*Cont.*):
    129, 138, 149, 156,
    165–166, 169, 172
complacency, *40*
composer, 41
compositions, 150–152
computers, 10, 13, 26, 28, 33,
    60, 64, 92, 94, 98–100,
    109–111, 113–114,
    142–143
Concorde, 85
conservatism, *39*
conservative, 33, 37–38, 81, 127
consulting, 1, 3, 20, *21*, 28, 69, 73
convolution, 115
Cooper, 120, 185
cooperation, 83, 86
core competencies, 29, 34, 38, 75
cost-benefit analysis, *44*
cost-driven, *42*
counterattack, 117, 119,
    120–121, 125, 130, 172
Cray, 28
creativity, 30, 34, 37, 54, 62, 79,
    149, 152, 157, 165
cross-discipline, 2, 6, 31, 38, 79,
    85, 102, 159, 164
crusader, 54
Cuba, 66
culture-driven, *42*
customers, 53, 75–76, 78, 118,
    160, 174
cyclical variation, 26, 78

da Vinci, 53
Darwin, 85, 126
Darwinian, 10, 19, 83–84, 87,
    127, 169
Dataquest, 100

Dawkins, 87, 185
DC10, 95
deaths, *140*
debt, 21
DEC, 2, 9, 14, 20–21, 22, 28,
    53, 55, 60, **67**, **69–71**, **73**,
    76, **81**, **93**, **95**, 103,
    110–111, 115
  workforce of, 68
decentralization, 34, 39, 63, 68,
    70
defender's, 119–122, 125, 126,
    129
defense industry, 43
depression, 28, 35, 135
diffusion, 18, 84, 96
diffusion model, 18
discounts, *44*
diseases, 6, 18, 109
diversity, 26, 102, 162, 167
Divine comedy, 41
dogs, 43, 45
downsizing, 99, 160, 161
Drucker, 98, 120, 185
DuPont, 54, 64, 129

earthquakes, 20
econometric, 5, 61
economic cycle, 52, 61
economies of scale, 43, 113, 175
economy, 4, 18, 20, 28, 30–31,
    33, 36–38, 40, 46, 50–51,
    61, 64–65, 89–91, 97, 114,
    147, 160, 164, 175
  United States, 4, 18, 20, 28,
    30–31, 33, 36, 37–38, 40,
    46, 50–51, 61, 64–65,
    89–91, 97, 114, 147, 160,
    164, 175

EDS, 28, 54
elasticity, *44*
embryo, 97
employees, 50–51, 71, 74, 161
empowerment, 29, 34, 70, 75
energy, 61, 78, **136**, **138**, 146
  consumption, 26, 61–63,
    136–137
  kinetic, 26
  pent-up, 153
  potential, 26
  primary, 6, 109, 137, 146
enterprise, 27, 70, 159, 178, 183
entrepreneurs, 34, 39, 107, 164
entrepreneurship, 29–30, 36, 39,
    40, 54, 70–71, 73, 75, 79,
    81, 135, 160
environment, 28, 76, 84,
    111–112, 161
epidemiologists, 18
equilibrium, 57, 101, 138–140,
    142–144, 163
Europe, 64–65, 162
European Economic
    Community, 162
  markets, 74
European Union, 65
evolution, 12, 26, 43–44, 61, 67,
    76, 78, 89, 96, 110, 112,
    118, 130, 147, 149,
    152–153, 156, 163–164
  of the evolution, 83–87
  The Power of Strategic, 46
excellence, 33–34, 37, 39, 165

facelift, 39
facelifting, 38–39
fall, 27, **38–39**, 41, *44*, 73
Farrell, Christopher, 120

feedback, 7, 33, 45
fertility, 157
fetus, 97–98
film, *155*, 156
Fisher, J.C., 18
fluctuations, 32, 68
football players, 153
forecast, 9, 11, 12, 16, 74, 135,
    138, 141
Formula One, 147–148
Forrester, Jay, 1, 5, 63, 147, 177,
    185
FORTRAN, 143
Foster, Richard, 19, 120–121,
    178, 186
fountain pen, 123–126, *125*
Fourier, 97, 186
foxes, 30, 119
fractal, 57, 89–90
free will, 11, 74, 147
fundamental change, *39*

Gaia, 86, 180, 186
gas molecules, 136
Gause, George, 119
gedanken experiment, 51
General Electric, 18
generalists, *39*
Genesis, 84
Gleick, James, 57, 186
Globalization, 162
GNP, 36, 50
God, 84, 87
gold, 40, 80, 83
Gorbachev, Mikhail, 65
Gray, Asa, 85
Greece, 46, 132
    ancient, 102

Greece (*Cont.*):
    mobile-telephone market, *121*,
        122
Growth Dynamics, 6, 13, 44, 46,
    88, 106, 167, 172, 179, 180

Handy, Charles, 3, 19, 24, 73,
    178, 186
hardware, 28, 69, 71, 73, 76, 98,
    123, **142–143**, 163
harmonic, 24, 25, 28, 103
    fundamental, 97
Harvard, 63, 178, 179, 181, 187
Harvard Business Review, 115,
    159, 181, 185
heart attack, 148
Hemingway, 153, *154*, 182
Henderson, Bruce, 43, 46
Heraclitus, 83
hi-fi, 101
highway, 13, 148
Hitchcock, *155*
Hitchcock, Alfred, 155–157
Hoechst, 64
holidays, 20
homeostasis, 138, 144, 163
horses, 19, *20*, 22, 23, 117
hypersonic, 162

IBM, 2, 20–21, 22, 28, 33, 64,
    73, 81, 100
IIASA, 9, 114
improvement, continuous, *39*
industry curve, 43, 175
infant mortality, 25, 30, 35–36,
    60
inflation, 36, 38, 40, 50, 101, 112

information technology, 98, 144
innovation, 39
*Innovation: The Attacker's
    Advantage*, 19, 178
innovations, 35, 63, 85, 133
instinct, 5, **103, 105, 106–108**
integration, vertical, 29, 39, 69,
    76, 81
Intel, 20–22, 60
Intermediation, 161
International Institute of
    Forecasters, 5
Internet, 28, 114, 175
intuition, 1, 105–107
invariants, 138–139, 142
investments, 31, 36, 48–50, 68,
    76
Italy, 17, 141

Japan, 141
just-in-time:
    action, 3
    innovation, 24
    replacement, **25–26**, 31

kefir, 120
Kelly, Kevin, 85, 86, 180, 186
Kleinschmidt, E.J., 120, 185
knowledge technology, 98
Kondratieff, Nikolai D., 28, 179

leadership, 29, 37, 39, 53, **65**,
    67, 104, 161, 164–165
learning, *39, 40*
learning curve, 109, 111,
    113–114, 152

legislation, 140
life cycle, 2, 4, 12–13, **14, *15*,**
    25, 27, 31, 32, 44, 47, 52,
    54, 66, 67, 71, 78, 81,
    89–91, 94–96, 104–105,
    114, 150, 165–166, 181
    shortening of, 92, 93
    shrinking, 92
Lotka, A.J., 19, 28, 120,
    125–127, 178, 183, 186

Machiavelli, Niccolo, 29, 80
macho, 161
mainframes, 99–100, 109
Major, John, 146
management science, 9, 79, 85
Mandelbrot, Benoit, 57
Marchetti, Cesare, 9–11, 84,
    137, 149, 177–180, 182,
    186
Margulis, Lynn, 84–85, 186
market niche, 10, 14, 16, 25, 31,
    48, 58, 93, 118, 126, 129,
    133
market share, 37–38, 42, 43–44,
    72, 95, 111–112, 120, 122,
    126, 133, 138, 170
market value, 22
marketers, 14, 16, 22–23, 148
marketplace, 2, 14, 28, 30, 71,
    100, 124, 133
Marshall, Alfred, 33
MBA, 159, 161
MCI, 64
McKinsey, 19, 120
metrics, *44*
microprocessor, 35, 60, 94
Microsoft, 20–21, 22, 51, 54

Miller, Lawrence, 54–55, 186
miners, *145*, 146
minicomputer, *15*, 93, 115
mining, 4, 27, 146
MIPS, 109–111, 113
Mission Possible, 3, 19, 178
MIT, 1, 63, 186
mobile telephone, *121*, 122, 132
modularity, 162
monetary indicators, 61
Moscow, 65, 119
Mozart, 149–152, 154, 157, 182
mules, 19, *20*, 23
multimedia, 163
mutations, 35, 86
mutualism, 123

Nader, Ralph, 142
natural growth, 10–12, 14, *25*,
    26, *62*, 71, 79, 89, *90*, 103,
    114, 120, 138, 149–150,
    165–166
natural selection, 83, 85–87
NCR, 121
necklace, 159, 163
network:
    communications, 64, 69, 163
    computer, 98, 100
    railway, 28
neutralism, 123, 126
niche, 14, *15*, 24, 35
    capacity of, 118, 170, 172
    ecological, 10, 12, 14, 17, 19,
        118
    market, 10, 14, 16, 25, 31, 34,
        35, 48, 58, 93, 118, 126,
        129, 133
    micro-, 171
    product, 91

niche (*Cont.*):
    saturation, 31, 117
    size, *128*, 149, 172, 181
    two-competitor, 122, 127, 171
nomadic working, 160
nylon, 64, 129, *130*, 131

Oedipus, 46, *47*
oil, 18, 138, 146
    prices, 18
    shocks, 18, 146–147
operations, 42
opportunities, *44*
optimization, 104, 113, 147
order, *42*
overshoot, 59

Panafon, *121*, 122, 132
parallel processing, 143
pendulum, 25, 26, 58
pent-up demand, 59, 93, 153
    energy, 153
    productivity, 156
performing artist, 41
personal computers, 33, 60,
    99–100
philosopher, 41
philosopher's stone, 1, 80–81
PIMS, 104, 180
politics, 20, 65, 87
pollution, 36
portable computers, 28, 64
positive myopia, 87–88
precursor, 59–60
predator, 28, 117, 124, 138
predeterminism, 11
predictability, 2–3, 12, 135, 149,
    165, 167

Predictions, 2, 13, 19, 26, 62–63, 145, 156, 177–182, 186
prey, 28, 117, 122, 124, 133, 138
price wars, *44*
price elasticity, 99, 173
pricing:
  as a science, *44*
  as an art, *44*
  commodity, *44*
  cross-border, *44*
  managers, *44*
pricing conference, *44*, 45, 106
product, 10, 14, 16, 23–25, 27–28, 30–31
  life cycle of, 9, **14**, *15*, 29
  phasing out, 14, 23
  portfolio, 4, 24
  service revenue of, 3
  subsitution of, 26
  substitution, 9, 20, 22, 24, **25**, 31
product lines, 69
product positioning, 112
productivity, 62, 79, 104, 133, 149–151, 153, 156
profitability, 31, 67, 71, 75–77
prophet, 54, 88
Pry, R.H., 18, 178, 185

question marks, 43, 45
questionnaire, 7, 45, 50–51, 53, 80, 105

R&D, 31, 36, 164
ROI, 50
rabbits, 13, 14, 16, 17–18, 118–119, 122

race, 66, 147–148
Rand, 141
random motion, 136
rationale, **103**, 105–107, 180
rebirth, 78, 153
recession, 38, 52, 92
reengineering, *39*, 117, 181
renewal, 157
Revue Française de Gestion, 159, 183
Rhone-Poulenc, 64
riddle, 46, 47
RISC, 26, 110–111
rocket, 67
romance, 105
rumors, 18
Russia, 65–67

safety, *140*
satire, 41
satisfaction, *44*
saturation, 93
SBU, 35, 44, **70**
scenario planning, multiple (shell), 4
scenarios, *62*, 88, 129, *130*, 131
scientific method, 6, 10–11, 136
S-curves, 12, *15*, 16, *17*, 18, 20–22, 24, 36, 83–84, 88–89, *90*, 91, 97, 114–115, *137*, 140, 144, *145*, 165, 177
  cascading, 83–84, *90*
  chaos and, 58, 144
  derivatives of, 48, *49*
  deviations from, *59*
  energy substitution and, 137
  invariants and, 141, 144
  levels of, 36–37

S-curves (*Cont.*):
multiple competitors and, 117,
    132
  personal achievement, and,
      149, 153–154, 156–157
  product positioning and,
      108–110, 112
  seasons and, 36–37
  of services, 114
  shortening of life cycles and,
      91, 92, 93, 94–95, 96, 101
  UK coal and, 147
seasons, 32, *39, 49*
  metaphor of, 30, 54–55, 67,
      70, 74, 80, 101, 165, 167
  negative, *68*
seat belts, *140*
segmentation, 32, 34, 39, 63, 65,
    68, 73, 171
selection, 31, 35, 84, 86–87
  natural, 83, 85–87
service life cycle, 114
Shakespeare, 40
Shanghai, 79
shares, 19, 20, 33, 40, 52, 117,
    137
  outstanding, 21
sheep, 118, 122
Shell, 4, 88
Shelley, Percy B., 27
Shevardnadze, Eduard, 65
Sigmoid curve, 3, 19, 24
Simon & Schuster, 13, 178, 180,
    185, 188
sine wave, 25
sine-wave, 25
Singapore, 79
Slywotzky, Adrian, 3, 21, 55,
    178, 179, 187
SME, 163

Smitalova, Kristina, 122, 181, 187
social security, 162
software, 26, 28, 45, 60, 69, 98,
    106, 108, 123, **142–143**,
    163, 172, 179
Soviet, 67
sparrows, 30
specialist, 31
specialists, 31–32, 36–38, 39,
    68, 164
speed:
  cameras, 124
  cars, 48, 50, 140–141
  computers, 109
  Unsafe at any, 142
Sperry, 72
sphinx, 47
spring, 27–28, 31, 34–35, 36,
    40–41, 44, 46, 51–52, 55,
    68, 71, 73–74, 76, 79, 82,
    91, 105, 135, 144, 157, 166
  negative, 68
Sputnik, 66
stars, 43, 45
steel industry, 38
stock market, 28, 49
stock rating, 50
stockholders, 50–51, 161
stocks, 36
stove pipes, 37, 69, 75, 164
strategic accounts, 38
strategic management, 2, 104
strategic performance monitor,
    103–104, 107
strategic planning, 2, 163
strategist, 103, 133
strengths, 44
substitution model, 10
suicide, 153–154
Sujan, Stefan, 122, 181, 187

summer, 27, 28, 30, 33–34, 37,
    38, 40–41, 44, 45, 51, 53,
    55, 58, 60, 64, 71, 73–76,
    77, 78, 81, 91, 105, 107,
    144, 147–149
  negative, 67, 70, 145, 147
superjumbos, 95
supersonic, 85, 96
Sweden, 141
Swiss, 102
symbiosis, 85, 123
System Dynamics, 5, 63, 177,
    186–187

Tandy, 28
teaching, 40
Telestet, 121, 122, 132
television, 63, 122, 155, 156
teleworking, 160
Tell, William, 108
The Age of Paradox, 19, 73, 178
thermodynamics, 136
tools, 36, 45, 103–104, 107–108,
    165, 167, 172, 179
  interactive, decision-support,
    etc., 2, 4, 5, 7, 13, 46, 80
total quality, 29, 37, 75
TQM, 33, 37, 39
tragedy, 41, 105
transience, 3
transition, 44
transportation, 144
  means of, 6, 10, 109, 147, 162
traveling, 48, 142, 144
Tristar (Lockheed), 95
turning point, 3, 38, 73

UK, 4, 27, 64, 145, 147, 182

ulcer, 148
Unisys, 28
United States, 23, 26, 36, 40,
    43, 51, 53, 66, 74, 100,
    126, 171, 182
universal constant, 138
USSR, 66

vacations, 20
Value Migration, 3, 54
value-driven, 42
Van Gogh, 61
VAX, 15, 69, 94, 109, 115
    11/750, 14, 16, 23
    11/780, 115
    MicroVAX, 16, 23, 94, 111
    MicxroVAX, 94
vehicle, 23
vendor, 75, 77
VHS, 33
video terminals, 143
Vienna, 9
vision-driven, 42
Volterra-Lotka, 120, 125–127

Waghorn, Terry, 3, 19, 178
war, 19, 100, 137, 166
Waterman Le Mans, 126
wave, 25, 28, 63, 77, 161
weapons industry, 86
win-win, 123
winter, 3, 27, 30–31, 32, 34–35,
    40, 42, 44, 45–46, 52,
    54–55, 58, 60, 63, 67,
    70–71, 75–76, 77, 78–79,
    81, 91, 101, 104, 107, 144,
    149, 166
  negative, 147

wireless, 163
wolf, 132
women, 157
wool, 129, *130*, 131
work ethic, 39
world, third, fourth, 163

yeasts, 120
Yeltsin, Boris, 65
Yugoslavia, 65

Zenith, 51, 81, 164

ABOUT THE AUTHOR

Theodore Modis is founder and president of Growth Dynamics, a Geneva-based consulting organization for leading international companies. Prior to starting his own firm, Modis was a senior strategy consultant at Digital Equipment Corporation. An internationally recognized futurist, he has a Ph.D. in physics and is the author of *Predictions: Society's Telltale Signature Reveals the Past and Forecasts the Future.*

Questions may be addressed to

Theodore Modis
GROWTH DYNAMICS
http://www.growth-dynamics.com
2, rue Beau Site
1203 Geneva, Switzerland
Tel. 41-22-345-5624
Fax: 41-22-345-4354
e-mail: tmodis@compuserve.com